INFLUENCE AMPLIFIED

CAPTIVATE, CONNECT AND LEAD WITH EXECUTIVE PRESENCE & STRATEGIC STORYTELLING

BOB ROITBLAT

Copyright © 2025 by Bob Roitblat All rights reserved.

Thank you for purchasing an authorized edition of this book and for respecting copyright laws by not reproducing, scanning, or distributing any part of it in any form without the publisher's permission, except as permitted by U.S. copyright law. For permission requests, please contact the publisher, Manifest Destiny Press.

The events depicted in this work are presented as truthfully as the author remembers or has reconstructed them through research and interviews. For narrative purposes, some dialogue, characters, incidents, thoughts, and actions have been dramatized based on information from various sources. With the exception of public figures, any resemblance to actual persons, living or deceased, is purely coincidental. Similarly, any identification with actual places, buildings, or products is unintended and should not be inferred.

Neither the publisher nor the author is engaged in rendering legal or other professional services through this book. If expert assistance is required, the services of appropriate professionals should be sought. The publisher and author shall have neither liability nor responsibility to any person or entity with respect to any loss or damage caused directly or indirectly by the information in this publication.

Book Cover by author

First edition 2025

ISBN 978-0-9819519-7-3 (print)

ISBN 978-0-9819519-8-0 (digital)

Library of Congress Control Number - 2025903216

Visit the author's website at www.roitblat.com

The publisher is concerned with and committed to protecting the galaxy by using environmentally sound printing practices.

Dedication

This book is dedicated to everyone who has shaped my understanding of Executive Presence and presentation skills.

To Gary Sherman and Chuck Bowman, who guided me during my early days in the film business—you gave me my first lessons in storytelling and presence, whether you realized it or not.

To Patricia Fripp, whose professionalism and excellence as a speaker continue to set the bar impossibly high—thank you for being both an inspiration and an exemplar.

To the countless speakers I've had the privilege to observe, share a stage with, or coach, and to the clients who have invited me to speak—your trust and collaboration have been invaluable to my growth.

To my much smarter older brothers, Barry and Herb, whose wisdom I've shamelessly borrowed (and repurposed for my keynotes) to sound more insightful than I am.

And finally, to my wife, Dawn, who has worked tirelessly to keep me humble—a task that's surely deserving of its own award.

Table of Contents

Dedicated   *iii*

Introduction   *1*

Part One
Foundations of Executive Presence   *5*

Chapter One
Redefining Executive Presence: Develop Confidence, Communication, and Composure   *7*

Chapter Two
Authenticity Over Perfection: Build Trust and Lead with Impact   *11*

Chapter Three
Make Your Voice Count: Amplify Influence and Drive Decisions at the Leadership Table   *17*

Assessing Your Current Level of Executive Presence   *21*

Part Two
The Power of Storytelling in Executive Presence   *25*

Chapter Four
Stories That Stick: Harness Universal Themes to Connect and Inspire   *27*

Chapter Five
Emotional Readiness: Share Stories That Resonate Not Overwhelm   *35*

Part Three
Structuring Presentations for Impact   *39*

Chapter Six
Design Presentations That Deliver   *41*

Chapter Seven
Craft Presentations Like a Pro: How Lessons From a Classic Fable Can Amplify Your Impact   *61*

Chapter Eight
Keep It Fresh: 3 Techniques to Make Every Presentation Relevant and Memorable   *65*

Chapter Nine
How Tailored Presentations Inspire Action, Build Trust, and Drive Lasting Impact   *69*

Part Four
Humor and Emotional Connection   *75*

Chapter Ten
The Humor Bridge: Build Trust and Influence Through Strategic Laughter   *77*

Part Five
Leveraging Multi-Sensory Engagement   *81*

Chapter Eleven
Creating Multi-Sensory Presentations That Captivate and Inspire   *83*

Part Six
Story crafting   *87*

Chapter Twelve
Storytelling: The Bridge to Connection and Persuasion   *89*

Chapter Thirteen
Turn Your Life Lessons Into Universal Stories That Resonate   *93*

Chapter Fourteen
Emotional Arc and Depth in Business Storytelling   99

Chapter Fifteen
Discover the Storyteller Within: How Life's Tiny Moments Engage Your Audience   105

Chapter Sixteen
Leverage Critical Moments to Create Compelling Narratives   109

Chapter Seventeen
The Power of One: Strategic Stories Are About One Person   113

Chapter Eighteen
When Numbers Numb: The Art of Data Storytelling   117

Chapter Nineteen
The Myth of Short Attention Spans: It's Not Your Audience, It's Your Content   123

Chapter Twenty
Storytelling Like a Pro: Borrow Hollywood Techniques to Transform Your Impact   127

Chapter Twenty-one
What Sings from the Page May Feel Like a Drag on the Stage   131

Chapter Twenty-two
Beyond the Notes: How Music's Storytellers Can Elevate Your Next Presentation   135

Chapter Twenty-three
Challenging the 'Know, Like, and Trust' Model for Presenters   139

Chapter Twenty-four
Hook Your Audience From the Start With Powerful Openings   143

Chapter Twenty-five
Say More With Less: How to Craft Concise, Impactful Stories   149

Chapter Twenty-six
End With Impact: Craft Closings That Leave a Lasting Impression   151

Chapter Twenty-seven
Ditch the Clichés: Speak Boldly to Command Attention and Credibility   155

Chapter Twenty-eight
Excel in the Three-Act Structure: Build Stories That Drive Business Success   157

Part Seven
Dynamic Delivery   163

Chapter Twenty-nine
From Vocalizing to Captivating: Secrets from a Galaxy Far, Far Away   165

Chapter Thirty
Command the Room: Unlocking Executive Presence with the Six Ss   169

Chapter Thirty-one
Refining The 'Unspoken' Elements of Delivery   175

Chapter Thirty-two
Beyond Words: Use Vocal Shading to Captivate and Connect   179

Chapter Thirty-three
The Secret to Making Meaningful Eye Contact to Enhance Your Impact   183

Chapter Thirty-four
The Art of Heart-to-Heart Connection: Lessons from Robert Fripp — *189*

Chapter Thirty-five
Conversational Storytelling: The Secret to Deep Connection — *193*

Chapter Thirty-six
Speak with Authority, Silence the Doubt — *197*

Chapter Thirty-seven
Big Stage, Small Screen: Tailoring Your Presentation to the Medium — *201*

Chapter Thirty-eight
Secrets for Executives to Shine — *205*

Chapter Thirty-nine
Set the Stage for Success: Why Your Presentation Depends on More Than Just Content & Delivery — *211*

Part Eight
Lessons from the Stage — *215*

Chapter Forty
Crafting a TED-Worthy Talk: Insights from My Journey — *217*

Chapter Forty-one
The Three Speeches: Lessons from the Keynote Stage — *221*

Chapter Forty-two
Conquer Stage Fright with These Simple Tricks — *225*

Part Nine
Practice and Preparation — *229*

Chapter Forty-three
The Art and Science of Deliberate Practice: Elevating Your Professional Game — *231*

Chapter Forty-four
Speechmaking Secrets I Learned from a DIY Bathroom Makeover — *235*

Epilogue: The Journey Continues — *237*

Appendix A: Powerful Openers and Closers. — *241*

Appendix B: Outline for Crafting a Story: — *249*

Appendix C: Hand Gestures for Executive Presence and Presentation Skills — *253*

Appendix D: Secrets for Memorizing Text — *257*

About the author — *261*

Acknowledgements — *263*

Introduction

The First Time I Stepped Onto a Stage, I Wanted to Step Right Off

I wasn't ready—not even close.

When I launched my company in 1984, renting personal computers wasn't just a new venture; it was a leap into uncharted territory. The concept was so new that the rental industry association invited me to speak at their annual convention. Not because we fit the mold—far from it.

Our business model, margins, and offerings were unlike anything the industry had seen. I assumed that's what intrigued them. What I didn't realize was how unprepared I was to stand on that stage.

When I arrived, I learned I'd been booked on the main stage—in a 900-seat auditorium. My stomach sank. The room felt like an ocean, and I was a solitary swimmer barely staying afloat. I'd never faced an audience that size. Standing there, I felt like a tightrope walker frozen halfway across, unsure whether to inch forward or retreat to safety.

I clutched my notes like a lifeline. My hands shook, and my voice sounded like it belonged to someone else. No strategy. No structure. No polish. Just raw nerves and one goal: survive. I did—barely.

What stayed with me wasn't the fear or my inadequacy—it was the realization that I made it through. I didn't thrive. I may not have been inspiring. But I survived. And survival is where transformation begins.

Since that first presentation, I've relied on Executive Presence and storytelling skills in countless situations—pitching clients, navigating high-stakes meetings, persuading city councils, and even delivering a victim impact statement in court. My passion for speaking grew so deeply that, for a time, I acted in feature films and on television. And, for more than 30 years now, I've had the privilege of working as a professional speaker.and coach.

Looking back, I wish I'd had a guide—a resource like this book. Since it didn't exist, I wrote it.

A Resource I Never Had

Elevating executive presence isn't about just getting by—it's about leading with confidence, communicating with clarity, and inspiring action. It's the ability to engage, adapt, and connect so deeply that you don't just capture attention—you transform your audience. True leaders don't simply share information; they shape perspectives, influence behavior, and drive lasting change with real impact.

This book is the roadmap and toolkit I wish I'd had on that first stage. It's packed with actionable tools to elevate how you lead, communicate, and inspire. By the end, you'll know how to turn potential into performance, ideas into impact, and presence into influence.

Inside, you'll find a blend of personal stories, practical strategies, and evidence-based insights. Some ideas might challenge you—that's intentional. This isn't just about learning; it's about growth. Growth means pushing boundaries and rethinking what's possible.

One of the most valuable lessons you'll gain is balancing confidence with humility. Few leaders get it right, but those who do change the game. My hope is that this book helps you strike that balance.

Ultimately, this book is about more than speaking or presenting. It's about transformation—not just in how you show up for others, but in how you lead yourself.

What You'll Gain From This Book

This book is more than just a guide—it's a transformation toolkit designed to elevate your Executive Presence and amplify your influence. Here's what you'll gain:

1. Build a Strong Foundation in Executive Presence

- Learn to project confidence without arrogance, earning respect and trust from colleagues and stakeholders alike.
- Develop composure under pressure, becoming the steady hand others look to in times of uncertainty.
- Balance authority with approachability, fostering both respect and relatability.

2. Build Communication Skills That Captivate

- Developing Executive Presence and strategic storytelling empowers you to authentically connect, inspire action, and leave a lasting impact.
- Simplify complex concepts and deliver them with clarity, ensuring your message resonates with diverse audiences.
- Learn how to adapt your communication style to bridge cultural and generational divides.

3. Elevate Your Leadership Impact

- Cultivate authenticity, aligning your words, actions, and values to inspire trust and loyalty.
- Harness emotional intelligence to build deeper connections with your team, clients, and peers.
- Lead with vulnerability and humility, creating a culture of psychological safety that empowers others to excel.

4. Command the Room in Any Situation

- Develop presence that turns heads the moment you enter a room, even before you speak.
- Use non-verbal communication, including body language and tone, to reinforce your verbal messages.
- Respond with grace and confidence to high-stakes questions, objections, or challenges.

5. Amplify Your Influence Across The Organization

- Become the go-to leader others trust for guidance, collaboration, and decision-making.
- Learn how to align your leadership style with organizational goals to drive engagement and innovation.
- Build a legacy of lasting impact, inspiring the next generation of leaders.

6. Leverage Storytelling to Inspire Action

- Discover how to craft stories that move people to action, whether you're presenting to a boardroom or leading a team meeting.
- Blend data and narrative to create presentations that are both informative and emotionally resonant.
- Utilize storytelling to reinforce your vision and align others with your goals.

7. Navigate Challenges with Confidence and Grace

- Adapt to dynamic business environments by leveraging resilience and adaptability.
- Manage crises with poise, turning challenges into opportunities for growth and innovation.
- Learn how to influence and persuade without force, using the power of ideas and respect.

8. Achieve Long-Term Growth

- Implement practical exercises and tools to measure and refine your Executive Presence over time.
- Gain the skills needed to continuously evolve, ensuring your leadership remains relevant and impactful.
- Build a personal and professional brand that reflects your highest aspirations.

9. Build a Personal Legacy

- Align your leadership actions with your core values to create a lasting, meaningful impact.
- Champion causes and mentor the next generation, ensuring your influence extends beyond your immediate role.
- Shape a reputation that endures, defined by authenticity, integrity, and grace.

Part One
Foundations of Executive Presence

"Leadership is not about a title or a designation. It's about impact, influence, and inspiration."
— Robin S. Sharma[1]

When you think of Executive Presence, what comes to mind? A strong voice? A polished look? That magnetic ability to command attention the moment someone walks into a room? Sure, those elements matter—but they're just surface-level. Real Executive Presence isn't about appearances; it's about influence. And at its core, influence is what defines leadership.

Leadership isn't a title. It's not power. It's the ability to drive results and create lasting, meaningful change that leads to real results. If behavior isn't shifting—if people aren't thinking differently, acting differently, achieving different results—you're not influencing. And if you're not influencing, you're not leading. You're just talking.

Executive Presence is both the tool and the vehicle for intentional influence. It shapes conversations, inspires action, and drives sustainable change that delivers real impact. That's why it's not just a trait—it's a critical leadership competency.

In these chapters, we'll explore what sets exceptional leaders apart—how they cultivate authenticity, balance confidence with humility, and communicate with clarity and conviction. We'll break down the evolving definition of gravitas (spoiler: it's not just about commanding a room; it's also about grace). And we'll get into the nuances of leading in high-stakes environments, from the boardroom to the front lines.

---

1. Attributed without citation. Most likely an amalgam of thoughts from his book, <u>The Leader Who Had No Title: A Modern Fable on Real Success in Business and in Life</u>. Nigeria: Free Press, 2010.

Influence Amplified

What really matters isn't just being seen—it's what happens after you walk away. Did you spark a shift? Did you inspire action? Did you leave something better than you found it? If the answer is yes, that's influence. And that's leadership.

Chapter One

Redefining Executive Presence: Develop Confidence, Communication, and Composure

Executive Presence isn't about having the loudest voice or the highest title—it's about something much deeper. It's the moment you enter a room, and every face turns toward you—not out of obligation, but with respect, curiosity, and trust. This magnetic force, a seamless blend of confidence, composure, and communication, defines true Executive Presence. It's not about positions or commanding tones; it's about making an impact and inspiring action.

Core Traits of Executive Presence

Executive Presence is a tapestry woven from three essential threads: confidence, communication, and composure. These traits enable leaders to influence not by force, but through the power of ideas, earning trust and respect effortlessly. However, Executive Presence also demands cultural sensitivity. A direct communication style, praised in some cultures, might be perceived as abrasive in others. Leaders with true Executive Presence adapt, bridging cultural divides with empathy and understanding.

Building Confidence Through Authenticity

Confidence doesn't mean having all the answers; it's about navigating uncertainty with assurance. Leaders build confidence by staying true to their values and leading with integrity. Authenticity emerges when competence meets humility—when leaders demonstrate their skills while remaining open to feedback and learning. This authenticity builds trust, forming the bedrock of genuine leadership.

Effective Communication

Great leaders don't just communicate; they connect. They transform complex ideas into clear, relatable messages and use storytelling to spark emotion and inspire action. A story well-told can turn an abstract idea into a vivid, memorable call to action, bridging the gap between vision and execution.

> *"Just because you have a platform doesn't mean that what you're communicating is true, wise, or intelligent"*[2]

Composure in High-Stakes Situations

High-stakes moments test a leader's mettle. Executive Presence shines brightest in these situations. Leaders who remain composed, leveraging emotional intelligence to navigate pressure, reassure teams and stakeholders alike. Their adaptability and calmness create a ripple effect, turning chaos into clarity.

Legacy and Long-Term Impact

Executive Presence isn't just about the here and now; it's about shaping a legacy. Leaders with lasting impact align their actions with their values, mentor the next generation, and champion meaningful causes. Legacy is built not in bursts of brilliance, but in consistent, value-driven leadership.

Modernizing Executive Presence

The traditional gravitas of leadership has evolved. Today, the emphasis is on grace—a balance of poise, empathy, and inclusiveness, all grounded in humility. Graceful leaders blend confidence with vulnerability, resilience with adaptability. They foster collaboration, embrace diverse perspectives, and lead with authenticity and care. This shift reflects modern values and resonates with today's workforce.

Gary Burnison, CEO of Korn Ferry, emphasizes the multifaceted nature of grace in leadership:

> *"Each of the Five Graces captures a human trait that in the aggregate literally compose the word grace:* **Gratitude** *- that lifts our hearts and elevates our spirits;* **Resilience** *- what makes the impossible possible;* **Aspiration** *- we can make tomorrow different and better than today;* **Courage** *- not having 'no fear,' but rather to 'know fear';* **Empathy** *- meeting others where they are to understand who they are."*[3]

---

2. Old Yiddish saying
3. Gary Burnison. "The Five Graces of Life and Leadership." Korn Ferry. https://www.kornferry.com/insights/featured-topics/leadership/the-five-graces-of-life-and-leadership.

Business Impact of Executive Presence

Executive Presence isn't just about looking the part—it's about capturing hearts and minds to drive tangible business results, and create real, lasting change. The leaders who excel at it don't just command attention—they inspire trust, rally teams, and drive organizations forward. Their influence shapes cultures, fuels innovation, and turns vision into action. They don't just manage crises—they navigate them with clarity. They don't just attract top talent—they keep them engaged and invested. And they don't just make decisions—they make decisions that stick because they've earned the confidence of those around them. In short, Executive Presence is the force that turns leadership into impact.

Balancing Confidence, Humility, and Vulnerability

Confidence earns trust, humility earns respect, and vulnerability builds connection. Together, these qualities create an authentic and relatable leadership style. Leaders who openly acknowledge challenges while maintaining composure inspire loyalty and psychological safety within their teams.

Action Steps for Personal Development

Executive Presence isn't innate; it's cultivated. Here's how to build it:

1. **Cultivate Confidence**: Hone your expertise and seek feedback to reinforce your abilities.
2. **Excel at Storytelling**: Learn to craft narratives that connect emotionally and convey your vision.
3. **Enhance Composure**: Practice mindfulness or stress management techniques to remain calm under pressure.
4. **Embrace Feedback**: Regularly seek constructive input and reflect on your leadership style.
5. **Develop Graceful Leadership**: Balance authority with empathy and foster inclusiveness in all interactions.

Chapter Wrap-up

Executive Presence is the silent force that transforms ordinary leaders into extraordinary ones. It's not about perfection, but authenticity—the courage to lead with confidence, the humility to listen, and the vulnerability to connect. By embodying these qualities, leaders don't just command attention; they inspire action, build lasting trust, and leave an indelible legacy.

Chapter Two
Authenticity Over Perfection: Build Trust and Lead with Impact

Imagine standing before a room filled with expectant faces. The spotlight casts a warm glow, and your heart pounds in your chest. You're not just there to share a message; you're there to connect, to inspire, and to lead. The key to achieving all this? Authenticity.

"Be yourself, but always your better self."[4]

Authenticity in Presenting: Embracing Your True Self

Audiences are perceptive. They can sense when you're putting on a show. Authenticity isn't about theatrics or perfection; it's about bringing your best, most genuine self to the stage. This doesn't mean abandoning professionalism. Instead, it means refining how you speak and carry yourself to reflect your true essence.

Think of authenticity as a sculptor chipping away at the excess to reveal the brilliance beneath. When you embrace your unique strengths, you connect with your audience on a deeper level. They don't just hear your words; they feel your sincerity. Your story becomes their story, and your message resonates far beyond the stage.

The Role of Executive Presence: Balancing Confidence and Genuineness

Executive Presence is the art of aligning your outward appearance, communication style, and inner confidence. It's not just about looking the part, but embodying it. True Executive Presence begins with genuineness. When your words, actions, and demeanor align, you captivate those around you.

Imagine Executive Presence as a tapestry woven with threads of authenticity. Each gesture, pause, and word contributes to the bigger picture. Your inner confidence—the belief in your message and yourself—shines through, creating a magnetic pull that draws others in.

---

4. Sentence-Sermons from Brigham Young University Quarterly. The Latter-Day Saints' Millennial Star, Volume 70, 1908.

Strengthening Authentic Presence: Practical Steps

Building authenticity requires intentional effort. Start by reflecting on your strengths. What makes you unique? Let these qualities shine in your delivery. Simplify your approach—strip away unnecessary theatrics and focus on clear, heartfelt communication.

Gestures matter, too. Align your body language with your words to create harmony in your message. Seek feedback from trusted peers to fine-tune your presence. And remember, every word, every movement should reflect the real you—a version refined, not fabricated.

Overcoming the Challenges of Impostor Syndrome

Even the most seasoned presenters grapple with imposter syndrome and other head trash.[5] That nagging voice in your head—*"You're not good enough"*—can be deafening, but it doesn't have to define your actions. True confidence lies in embracing vulnerability, not hiding behind a mask.

Take Richard, a coaching client, for example. He was consumed by thoughts like, *"People will realize I don't know how to speak, I don't know enough about my topic, or I haven't practiced enough."* Overwhelmed by self-doubt, he donned a metaphorical mask and adopted a contrived storyteller persona—**Speakerman!**—a caricature of what he thought a presenter should be. Yet, the genuine connection he longed for remained elusive.

Everything changed when Richard let go of the façade and chose to speak authentically. By embracing his imperfections and speaking from the heart, his message began to truly resonate. Vulnerability isn't a weakness; it's the bridge that forges genuine connection with your audience.

---

5. 'Head trash' is a colloquial expression rather than a well-documented phrase with a specific originator. It is used to describe the persistent, negative thoughts, self-limiting thoughts, or self-doubt that people experience. An alternative is Psychic Debris. References include: Mackay, Harvey. Dig Your Well Before You're Thirsty: The Only Networking Book You'll Ever Need. United Kingdom: Crown, 1999. The Eight Biggest Mistakes Personal Trainers Make. N.p.: Fitness Together Franchise, (n.d.). 2007. Dump Your Head-Trash Journal. N.p.: Caboodle Marketing, Incorporated, 2008.

Authenticity vs. Perfection: Why Realness Wins

Audiences value authenticity over polish. They don't need a perfect presenter; they need a real one. Sharing your struggles and triumphs creates a bond that transcends the stage. Vulnerability humanizes you, making your message relatable and memorable.

Building Trust Through Authenticity

Trust is the foundation of leadership, and authenticity is the cornerstone of trust. When your words align with your actions, you create a sense of reliability and integrity. Share your story—the victories and the setbacks. Let your audience see your humanity.

Authenticity fosters relatability. When people see themselves in your story, they feel connected and understood. This emotional connection drives loyalty and inspires action.

The Negative Impact of Inauthenticity

Inauthenticity, even unintentional, erodes trust. Misaligned cues—a forced smile, a mismatched tone—create unease. Your audience may not consciously register these signals, but they sense them.

Body language and tone amplify your message, which we discuss further in Part Seven. Ensure they complement, rather than contradict, your words. Authenticity is a symphony where every element—posture, gestures, voice—works in harmony to convey your truth.

Developing Authentic Leadership

Authenticity in leadership begins with self-awareness. Reflect on your values and align your actions with them. Transparency and active listening are vital. Share your intentions openly, even when decisions are tough. Authentic leaders value input and foster collaboration, building trust and engagement.

Authenticity as a Leadership Foundation

Leading with authenticity creates a virtuous cycle. Trust builds influence. Influence fosters engagement. Engagement drives innovation. When leaders are authentic, they empower others to take risks, contribute, and grow.

Imagine your authenticity as the roots of a tree. Deep and grounded, it supports every branch of your leadership. It's the unseen force that sustains trust, loyalty, and impact.

Practical Steps to Cultivate Authenticity

Start by identifying inconsistencies in your words and actions. Address these gaps to strengthen your credibility. Practice emotional awareness—understand how your feelings influence your communication.

Share personal anecdotes to illustrate your values and experiences. Model vulnerability to show that being real is a strength, not a weakness. These steps help you connect authentically, leaving a lasting impression.

Chapter Wrap-up: The Authentic Path Forward

Authenticity isn't just a strategy; it's a way of being. When you embrace your true self and lead with authenticity, you inspire others to do the same. Your words become more than messages; they become moments of connection, trust, and transformation.

So, the next time you step onto the stage or into a leadership role, remember this: Your authenticity is your greatest asset. Let it shine, and watch as it lights the way for others.

Action Steps:

1. Reflect on your core values and identify how they align with your words and actions. Use this clarity to ensure consistency in your communication.

2. Practice speaking from the heart by sharing a personal anecdote in your next presentation. Let your story illustrate your values.

3. Seek feedback from colleagues or mentors on how authentic your communication feels. Use their insights to refine your approach.

4. Observe your body language and tone during your next leadership moment. Ensure they align with the message you want to convey.

5. Embrace vulnerability by acknowledging challenges or mistakes in your journey. Show your team that being real builds stronger connections.

6. Incorporate emotional awareness into your daily interactions. Recognize how your emotions influence your tone and delivery.

7. Build trust by being transparent about your intentions, even when making tough decisions. Transparency strengthens credibility.

8. Regularly reflect on moments of misalignment between your actions and values. Identify ways to address and prevent these inconsistencies.

Chapter Three

Make Your Voice Count: Amplify Influence and Drive Decisions at the Leadership Table

You've made it. After years of dedication, strategy, and growth, you've earned your spot at the C-suite table. But being there is only the beginning. In the high-stakes environment of executive leadership, it's not just about having a seat—it's about ensuring your voice carries weight, shapes decisions, and inspires action.

Influence at this level isn't about how loudly you speak; it's about how effectively you communicate. Let's explore how to make your presence felt in ways that drive meaningful impact.

The Art of Being Heard

C-suite discussions are a unique challenge. Every conversation moves quickly, and every statement must add value. Here's how to ensure your contributions stand out:

1. Listen Actively

The first rule of influence is understanding the dynamics of the room. Pay attention not just to what is said, but how it's said. Decode the underlying concerns, motivations, and power dynamics shaping the conversation. Active listening isn't passive—it's a tool to position your insights with precision.

2. Speak with Purpose

Every word counts in the C-suite. Avoid rambling or generic statements. Instead, focus on delivering concise, well-structured contributions that address specific challenges or opportunities. Lead with your key point and back it up with evidence or a compelling narrative.

3. Transform Data into Stories

Data is powerful, but stories make it unforgettable. Instead of reciting numbers, craft a narrative around them. For example, instead of saying, *"Our customer satisfaction rate increased by 15%,"* you might say, *"This 15% jump reflects the loyalty of customers who now trust our product to meet their needs."* Stories contextualize data, making it relatable and emotionally resonant.

4. Command the Room with Presence

Your body language, tone, and energy are just as important as your words. Sit with confidence, make deliberate eye contact, and vary your tone to emphasize key points. When you project poise and authority, others are more likely to listen and engage.

Balancing Assertiveness and Approachability

In the C-suite, balance is key. Over-assertiveness can alienate peers, while excessive deference may cause your voice to be overlooked. Assertiveness combined with approachability ensures your ideas are heard without overpowering the conversation.

- **Assertiveness:** Speak with conviction. Use clear, confident language and avoid qualifiers like *"I think"* or *"maybe."*
- **Approachability:** Invite collaboration. Phrases like *"What's your take on this?"* show you value others' input, fostering trust and teamwork.

Leverage Emotional Intelligence

Emotional intelligence (EQ) is a superpower in executive settings. Recognize the emotional undercurrents of the room and tailor your approach to resonate with others. Acknowledge differing perspectives, show empathy, and build consensus without compromising your convictions.

The Power of Brevity

Time is a precious commodity in the C-suite. Long-winded explanations dilute your impact. Structure your contributions to hit hard:

1. **Start Strong**: Lead with your main point.

2. **Be Direct**: Eliminate fluff and unnecessary details.

3. **End with Clarity**: Leave no ambiguity about your recommendation or takeaway.

Authenticity is Your Anchor

At this level, authenticity is non-negotiable. People can sense when you're posturing. Be genuine in your interactions, transparent in your intentions, and consistent in your actions. Authenticity fosters trust, which is the currency of influence.

Action Steps: Amplify Your Voice at the Table

Put these principles into action with these steps:

1. **Prepare Thoroughly**: Anticipate key topics and come with data-driven insights and solutions.

2. **Observe Dynamics**: Study how decisions are made and tailor your contributions accordingly.

3. **Practice Clarity**: Rehearse delivering your points succinctly and with confidence.

4. **Seek Feedback**: Ask peers or mentors how your presence is perceived and adjust as needed.

5. **Be Intentional**: Make every word and gesture count, ensuring your contributions align with the organization's strategic goals.

Chapter Wrap-up

Earning a seat at the C-suite table is an achievement. But making your voice resonate is the real mark of leadership. With preparation, clarity, and authenticity, you can shape decisions, inspire confidence, and leave a lasting legacy. Your presence isn't just about being in the room—it's about defining the future from that seat.

Assessing Your Current Level of Executive Presence

Questions for Self-Reflection

1. Confidence and Authenticity

- How well do I project confidence in high-stakes situations without coming across as arrogant?
- How well am I able to stay true to my values and lead with integrity, even under pressure?

2. Communication Skills

- How well do I clearly and concisely communicate complex ideas in a way that resonates with my audience?
- How effective am I at using storytelling to inspire and connect with others?

3. Body Language and Poise

- How well do I maintain strong, confident body language (eye contact, posture, gestures) that reinforces my verbal communication?
- How well do I stay composed and in control during crises or stressful situations?

4. Influence and Persuasion

- How well am I able to influence decisions and inspire action without resorting to force?
- How effective am I at persuading others through storytelling and engaging delivery?

5. Emotional Intelligence

- How well do I accurately read the emotions of others and adjust my communication style accordingly?
- How well do I manage my own emotions in high-pressure situations?

6. Gravitas

- How well do I project gravitas—an unspoken authority and seriousness that commands respect?
- How well do I lead discussions in a way that conveys weight without being overbearing?

7. Visionary Thinking and Adaptability

- How well am I able to see the big picture and align my team or organization with long-term goals?
- How well do I adapt to changing circumstances and adjust my leadership approach?

8. Connection and Relationship-Building

- How effective am I at building emotional connections with my team and stakeholders?
- How well do people see me as relatable and approachable while still respecting my authority?

9. Storytelling and Presenting

- How well am I able to captivate an audience during speeches or presentations?
- How effectively do I use stories to illustrate points and emotionally engage my audience?

10. Balancing Confidence with Vulnerability

- How well do I balance confidence with humility and vulnerability in my leadership style?
- How open am I to feedback and willing to show vulnerability when necessary?

Exercises for Developing Executive Presence

1. Body Language and Poise

- Observe your body language in a mirror or ask a colleague for feedback. Focus on maintaining eye contact and using purposeful gestures during your next presentation or meeting.

2. Influence and Persuasion

- Reflect on a recent negotiation or discussion where you needed to influence others. Did you rely more on facts or your ability to connect emotionally? Identify ways to improve your persuasive techniques.

3. Emotional Intelligence

- After your next high-stakes interaction, write down how you handled your emotions and how you responded to others' emotions. Evaluate whether you stayed calm and composed.

4. Gravitas

- Seek feedback from trusted colleagues or mentors on how they perceive your presence in meetings. Do they feel you project the right level of gravitas?

5. Visionary Thinking and Adaptability

- Reflect on a recent challenge or shift in your organization. How did you respond? Were you able to adjust your strategy to meet new demands?

6. Connection and Relationship-Building

- After your next interaction, evaluate how well you connected with others on a personal level. Did your communication foster trust and collaboration?

7. Storytelling

- Select a personal or professional experience and practice turning it into a compelling narrative. Focus on making it relatable and engaging by using emotional depth, vocal variety, and body language. Reflect on how your audience responds and adjust accordingly.

8. Presentation Delivery

- Record yourself delivering a short speech or presenting an idea. Focus on clarity, tone, pacing, and body language. After watching, assess if your confidence, composure, and delivery inspire trust and command attention. How clearly did you communicate your main points? Did you use storytelling techniques to engage your audience? Identify areas for improvement.

9. Vocal Variety

- Experiment with vocal shading and variety during presentations. Practice using different tones to emphasize points, add emotion, or maintain engagement. Evaluate if this enhances your influence and ability to captivate your audience.

10. Crisis Simulation

- Simulate a high-pressure situation where you must make a decision or deliver bad news. Pay attention to how well you maintain composure, clarity, and poise. Analyze your ability to stay calm and influence others in the face of adversity.

11. Non-Verbal Communication

- Practice using strong body language, including standing tall, making eye contact, and using purposeful gestures during presentations. Ask for feedback on whether your physical presence aligns with the confidence you aim to project.

12. Confidence

- List three recent interactions where you had to demonstrate confidence. Reflect on whether you remained authentic and how others responded to you.

By answering these questions and engaging in these exercises, you can gain deeper insights into your current level of Executive Presence and identify clear areas for growth.

Part Two

The Power of Storytelling in Executive Presence

Have you ever noticed how a well-told story can hold your attention longer than even the most compelling set of facts? Stories do more than deliver information—they ignite something deeper. They connect us emotionally, make complexity easier to grasp, and inspire action. As a leader, storytelling isn't just a skill—it's a superpower. It's the difference between being heard and being remembered. Executive presence gets people to listen. Stories get people to feel. And when people feel, they act. That's real influence.

Great leaders know that no single influence strategy is universally effective—just like no communication style works in every situation. What works in one moment might fall flat in another. The key isn't sticking to one approach; it's knowing when to pivot. When to persuade with logic. When to appeal to values. When to spark curiosity. And when to let silence do the talking.

Storytelling is powerful because it delivers multiple influence strategies at once, making messages more persuasive, memorable, and impactful.[6] A well-crafted story engages logic, emotion, and credibility simultaneously. It transforms abstract ideas into tangible experiences. It gives people a reason to care. And most importantly, it sticks. Facts fade, but stories stay with us.

In this section, we'll explore the transformative power of storytelling—why stories resonate more deeply than directives, how they amplify influence, and why pairing them with a dash of data is a winning strategy. You'll learn how to harness storytelling to build trust, inspire teams, and drive action. With practical insights and actionable steps, this section will help you turn your experiences into compelling narratives that engage, motivate, and leave a lasting impact.

Ready to unleash the storyteller within? Onward and upward!.

---

6. Storytelling is just one tool in the influence toolkit. While many individual strategies are highly effective, detailing them all falls outside the scope of this book.

Chapter Four

Stories That Stick: Harness Universal Themes to Connect and Inspire

Picture this: You walk into a crowded meeting room. The air hums with anticipation as you prepare to present your ideas. Instead of launching into a barrage of data points and technical jargon, you begin with a story. The room falls silent. Heads tilt forward, eyes focus, and the collective energy shifts. This is the transformative power of storytelling – the ability to captivate, connect, and inspire in ways no spreadsheet ever could.

Stories are more than entertainment; they're a fundamental part of human communication. From ancient campfires to today's boardrooms, storytelling bridges the gap between logic and emotion, fostering a deeper understanding and lasting impact. In business, where persuasion and clarity are paramount, this skill is not a luxury, but a necessity.

The Resonance of Stories Over Sermons

Stories don't demand; they invite. They open a window into experiences and emotions, allowing listeners to reflect and interpret without feeling dictated to. Sermons, in contrast, tell audiences what to think. A well-told story offers space for interpretation—something to think about—creating a personal connection that lingers long after the meeting ends.

Consider how stories touch universal themes like hope, resilience, and triumph. These aren't merely narratives; they're bridges that connect individuals across diverse backgrounds. A tale of overcoming adversity, for instance, resonates even if the specifics differ. It's about the shared human experience.

Matching Stories to the Moment:

Storytelling is not just about choosing a narrative; it's about selecting the *right* narrative and matching its *level of intimacy* to the moment. Storyteller Donald Davis often reflects on the rich tradition of storytelling that took place in different parts of the home—like the front porch, living room, or kitchen[7]—each setting inherently suggesting varying levels of emotional connection and audience trust.[8] While personal facts and stories can create powerful connections, problems arise when the level of intimacy shared exceeds the trust established. Authenticity and vulnerability are valuable, but do not come with an obligation to bare your soul to the world; they must be balanced with the audience's readiness to receive them.

- **Front Porch Stories**: These are shared openly with anyone, much like how neighbors might exchange tales on a porch in a small town. These stories are light, relatable, and perfect for building initial rapport with a broader audience.
- **Living Room Stories**: These are more personal, shared with a trusted circle—like close friends gathered in the modern living room or yesteryear's parlor. They carry a deeper emotional weight and require a level of trust and connection with the audience.
- **Kitchen Stories**: These are the most private and vulnerable, shared only with the closest of confidants. They delve into deeply personal experiences and require a profound level of intimacy and trust with the listener.

Choosing the right type of story is critical. Think of it like this: if the audience wouldn't trust you to watch their purse for a minute, it's too soon to share Living Room or Kitchen stories. Starting with a Front Porch story helps build the trust and connection needed to graduate to deeper, more intimate narratives.

---

7. See: Donald Davis, Telling Your Own Stories: For Family and Classroom Storytelling, Public Speaking, and Personal Journaling. United States: August House, 1993. Davis, Donald. How They Linger: Stories of Unforgettable Souls. N.p.: Parkhurst Brothers Publishers Incorporated, 2024.
8. Dietz and Silverman supply the categorization in: Karen Dietz, Lori L. Silverman, Business Storytelling For Dummies. Germany: Wiley, 2013. P. 249, based on Davis's work.

Strategic Storytelling in Action

When crafting your message, consider the following steps to align your storytelling with your audience's needs:

1. **Assess the Relationship**: Is this audience encountering you for the first time, or do they already trust you as a leader? For new audiences, Front Porch stories are a safe starting point.

2. **Match the Moment**: If you're addressing a smaller, more familiar group—like a team you've worked with closely—Living room stories can add an emotional depth that resonates. For one-on-one mentoring or deeply personal lessons, a kitchen story might create a powerful and lasting impact.

3. **Gauge the Stakes**: The level of intimacy should align with the stakes of your message. A keynote presentation calls for stories that inspire and connect universally, while a smaller workshop might benefit from more vulnerability.

Building Trust Through Storytelling

The key takeaway from Davis's framework is the importance of aligning the level of story intimacy with your audience's readiness. Leaders who share stories that are too personal too soon risk alienating their listeners. Conversely, leaders who hesitate to deepen the connection when the moment calls for it miss opportunities to inspire action and build loyalty.

> *"The age-old practice of storytelling is one of the most effective tools leaders can use. But they need to pick their stories carefully and match them to the situation."*[9]

As Davis's framework shows, storytelling is a journey of trust. Start where your audience is, and guide them toward deeper connection with purpose and care.

---

9. Stephen Denning, "Telling Tales," Harvard Business Review (May 2004) p. 122-129

The Power of 'Why'

Why do you do what you do? Answering this question isn't just an introspective exercise—it's the foundation of effective storytelling. Sharing your 'why' transforms a presentation from a mere data dump into an inspiring journey. It shifts the focus from telling people what to believe to showing them what drives you. This subtle yet powerful shift builds trust, sparks curiosity, and fosters genuine engagement—the first step toward meaningful influence.

When you share your motivations, struggles, and insights, your story becomes a gift—an open invitation for your audience to explore and connect. People resonate not with what you do, but with why you do it. That connection inspires them to follow willingly, not just comply.

Your 'why' isn't just a reason; it's a bridge that links your purpose to your audience's hearts and minds, turning simple communication into lasting impact.

The Neuroscience of Storytelling

Something remarkable happens when we hear a story. Our brains synchronize with the storyteller's. The joy, fear, or excitement they convey becomes our own. This isn't poetic; it's scientific. Storytelling activates multiple areas of the brain, transforming passive listening into active participation.

Audiences become collaborators in the narrative, filling in details, imagining scenarios, and feeling every twist and turn. This shared experience isn't just engaging—it's unforgettable.

Relatability and Memory

Good stories are both personal and universal. While the specifics might vary, the emotional truths they carry—perseverance, elation, loss—connect us all. This is why facts fade, but stories endure. Our brains prioritize narratives because they imbue information with depth and emotion.

A story about a team's struggle to meet a deadline will stick far longer than a bullet point about productivity. Wrapped in a compelling narrative, information becomes vivid, relatable, and memorable.

Building Collective Identity

Movements, brands, and teams thrive on shared stories. Think of the civil rights movement or Apple's journey from near collapse to global dominance. These narratives don't just inform; they unite. They shape identity and inspire collective action, whether in social causes or corporate missions.

In business, storytelling shapes culture. Leaders who share authentic stories about values and successes create alignment and motivation. A story isn't just about where you've been; it's a vision of where you can go together.

Business Storytelling: Data Meets Drama

In a world awash with data, stories give numbers context and meaning. *"Sales grew 20%"* informs; a story about how a team overcame challenges to achieve that growth inspires. Data provides clarity, but storytelling drives action.

Strategic storytelling blends authenticity with purpose. It's not just about recounting events; it's about guiding your audience to a conclusion or action. Stories humanize information, making it relatable and compelling.

Authenticity and Integrity

Audiences crave authenticity. They can sense when a story is crafted for effect rather than rooted in truth. The most impactful stories align with your values and reflect genuine experiences. Transparency and integrity aren't optional; they're essential.

Ethical storytelling also builds trust. Exaggeration might win short-term attention, but authenticity fosters lasting credibility. The best leaders tell stories that are as honest as they are inspiring.

Resilience and Learning From the Past

The most powerful stories often stem from adversity. They're tales of resilience, adaptability, and triumph over challenges. These narratives don't just inspire; they teach. They provide blueprints for navigating uncertainty and setbacks.

As you reflect on your own journey, think about the lessons hidden in your history. Stories of past crises and recoveries aren't just anecdotes; they're tools for the future.

Action Steps:

1. **Discover Your Story**: Reflect on your personal 'why.' Write a one-paragraph story that authentically communicates your purpose and motivation. Focus on what drives you and how it connects to your audience.

2. **Adapt Stories to Context**: Select one universal theme (e.g., resilience, growth, triumph) and tailor a story to different levels of intimacy (Front Porch, Living Room, or Kitchen). Practice aligning the story with varying audience dynamics.

3. **Transform Data Into Drama**: Identify a key fact or statistic you regularly present. Craft a short narrative around it that highlights the human effort or emotions behind the numbers, to make it both relatable and unforgettable.

4. **Shape Collective Identity**: Create a signature story for your team or organization that embodies your shared culture, mission, or values. Share it at your next meeting or presentation to build alignment and foster connection.

5. **Incorporate Story-Driven Action**: Design your next presentation with a clear storytelling arc. End with a call to action tied directly to the story's message, inspiring your audience to take tangible steps.

6. **Test and Iterate**: Share your crafted stories with a small, trusted group. Gather feedback on clarity, emotional impact, and authenticity. Revise and refine to ensure they resonate with broader audiences.

By embracing storytelling, you transform information into inspiration and connection. You don't just communicate; you lead. Harness this power, and watch as your words leave an indelible mark.

Chapter Five

Emotional Readiness: Share Stories That Resonate Not Overwhelm

Telling a story that holds emotional weight can be one of the most powerful tools in a leader's arsenal. Stories that tap into shared human experiences—loss, triumph, hope, resilience—forge connections that transcend barriers. But the ability to share such stories effectively hinges on one key factor: emotional readiness. In the last chapter we talked about the audience's emotional readiness. In this chapter we talk about yours.

When a storyteller brings their audience to the brink of tears or inspires deep reflection, the impact can be transformative. However, if the storyteller themselves becomes overwhelmed by their emotions, the focus shifts. Instead of guiding the audience through the narrative's emotional depths, they may unintentionally draw attention to their personal vulnerability, disrupting the message's clarity.

The Role of Vulnerability in Leadership

Vulnerability is a celebrated leadership trait because it builds trust and connection. In storytelling, however, unresolved vulnerability can overwhelm the narrative. If visible distress or emotional loss of control occurs, the audience's focus may shift from the story's message to the storyteller's emotional state. The storyteller's role is to remain composed, ensuring the story's impact stays with the audience rather than being overshadowed by the presenter's emotions.

A Personal Reflection on Emotional Readiness

Ever since my mother passed away in 2009, I've wanted to tell the story of how I had to decide whether to authorize significant medical procedures that might prolong her life for a few days—just enough time for my middle brother to see her alive one last time—or make her comfortable and let her pass peacefully.

The burden fell on me because my oldest brother, who had medical power of attorney, was boarding a plane when the hospital called, and they needed immediate direction.

One of the deciding factors was a conversation my mother and I had many years earlier about not wanting to live as a vegetable. Neither of us liked broccoli, so we especially didn't want to be a broccoli. But the most gut-wrenching issue for me was the realization that I would never have the chance to repair our relationship, which had deteriorated over the previous ten years.

I've tried to tell this story twice and couldn't make it through. I don't know if I'll ever be ready, but the experience has taught me a valuable lesson about emotional readiness. Stories like this demand more than courage; they require reflection, processing, and the ability to convey the message without being overcome by unresolved feelings.

The Power of Balance

Emotion is the lifeblood of storytelling. It makes narratives memorable, relatable, and impactful. Yet, there's a fine line between showing genuine emotion and becoming consumed by it. A storyteller who is overly emotional risks losing the audience's focus on the story's takeaway. Instead, the audience may become preoccupied with the storyteller's feelings, diluting the intended message.

Processing emotions beforehand is the key to achieving this balance. When a storyteller has worked through their feelings about the story, they can share it with clarity, control, and confidence. This doesn't mean stripping the narrative of its emotional depth; instead, it ensures the storyteller can channel that emotion into a compelling and authentic delivery.

Signs You're Ready—Or Not

How do you know if you're ready to share a deeply emotional story? The litmus test is simple: If you can tell the story without it bringing tears to your own eyes, you're likely prepared to guide your audience through the journey. Emotional readiness doesn't mean being indifferent or detached; it means being grounded enough to deliver the story's impact without being swept away.

If you find yourself still emotionally overwhelmed, consider this a signal to pause. Reflect, process, and revisit the story when you're in a stronger emotional place. The best stories come from a place of understanding and readiness, empowering both the storyteller and the audience.

Crafting Emotional Impact Without Losing Control

To excel in the art of emotionally impactful storytelling, consider these strategies:

1. **Rehearse with Reflection:** Practice telling your story aloud. If emotions bubble up, pause and reflect on why. Rehearsing allows you to gauge your emotional state and refine your delivery.

2. **Anchor the Message:** Focus on the lesson or takeaway your story conveys. This helps ground your emotions and keeps the narrative centered on its purpose.

3. **Use Emotional Cues Strategically:** Vocal inflections, pauses, and gestures can amplify the emotional impact without requiring tears or visible distress. Let your delivery convey the depth of your story.

4. **Seek Feedback:** Share your story with trusted colleagues or mentors before presenting it publicly. Their observations can help you fine-tune the balance between emotion and composure.

Why Emotional Readiness Matters

Emotionally charged stories are transformative because they connect us on a human level. But for the connection to be truly effective, the storyteller must be ready to guide the audience with confidence and clarity. When a leader shares an emotional story from a place of readiness, they build trust, inspire action, and leave a lasting impression. This balance ensures the audience feels the story's weight—not the storyteller's unresolved pain.

As you refine your storytelling craft, remember: powerful stories aren't just about what you share—they're about how you share it. When you're ready, your audience will be too.

Part Three
Structuring Presentations for Impact

Standing on a stage, you face a choice: will you present a collection of facts, figures, and data points, or will you ignite a movement? Great presentations aren't just about what you say—they're about what your audience feels, remembers, and acts on after you leave the room.

In Parts One and Two, we examined the core elements of Executive Presence—confidence, authenticity, and composure—and how these traits inspire trust, influence decisions, and forge lasting connections. We also explored the transformative power of storytelling in leadership, honing how narratives can simplify complexity, evoke emotion, and amplify impact. Now, we shift into the art and science of crafting presentations that do more than engage—they create lasting impressions.

From stepping into the role of an Oracle who inspires action to avoiding content overload and captivating diverse audiences, you'll discover strategies to ensure your message resonates. Whether it's tailoring content for maximum relevance or harnessing timeless storytelling principles, this section equips you to leave a powerful and lasting impression every time you speak. Ready to elevate your presentations to the next level? Then onward it is!

Chapter Six
Design Presentations That Deliver

Close your eyes and picture this: You're standing before an audience, their eyes fixed on you, hanging on your every word. Your ideas flow effortlessly, painting vivid pictures and evoking powerful emotions. Each sentence draws them closer to a profound realization. This isn't luck or raw talent—it's the product of a meticulously crafted presentation framework, well-told stories, and dynamic delivery techniques designed to captivate, inspire, and deliver with precision.

The Anatomy of an Effective Presentation Framework

Crafting a memorable presentation is like building a house. Each part of the framework is essential, working together to create a cohesive and dynamic whole. Let's break it down, brick by brick.

Assembling a Presentation Using Modules

A great presentation isn't written in a straightforward, start-to-finish progression. Instead, it's constructed using five key building blocks or modules. Each module is a self-contained element, giving your presentation both flexibility and adaptability. In essence, you don't so much write a presentation as assemble it from these distinct, purposeful modules:

1. **Opening**: First impressions are everything. Your audience's attention is at its peak during the first 30 seconds, making this your golden opportunity to captivate them. This is where the 'HOT OPENING' comes into play *(see more on page 143)*—a bold, attention-grabbing action, statement or story that answers the audience's two most pressing questions: *Why should I care?* and *Why should I trust you?* Think of it as the spark that ignites curiosity and sets the tone for the entire presentation.

Introducing Objectives: Setting the Stage for Success

Imagine walking into a forest without a map, unsure of where you're headed or why you're there. Now imagine being handed a trailmap—a clear, detailed guide that lays out your journey step by step. That's the power of sharing objectives at the start of your presentation.

When you provide a structure for your presentation, you give your audience more than just information—you give them clarity and purpose. Objectives serve as a roadmap, defining your goals and guiding both you and your audience toward a shared destination.

Why Share Objectives?

Setting the tone with clear objectives does more than organize your thoughts—it transforms the audience's experience. Here's how:

- **Creates Anticipation**: Sharing your goals upfront allows the audience to mentally prepare for the journey ahead. They know what to expect and are more likely to stay engaged.
- **Increases Retention**: People remember information better when they understand its purpose. Objectives act as signposts, helping your audience connect the dots between your message and their own needs.
- **Keeps You Focused**: As a presenter, objectives keep you on track, ensuring your message stays purposeful and on point.
- **Opens the Door for Feedback**: By outlining your goals, you invite the audience to evaluate your success, providing you with valuable insights for improvement.

Creative Ways to Introduce Objectives

The way you introduce your objectives can set the tone for your entire presentation. While you can simply state them after your opening—*"I have three objectives today..."*—why not make them more dynamic and memorable? Here are a few ideas:

A. Pose a Question

Kick off with a question that sparks curiosity and leads naturally to your objectives:

- *"Have you ever wondered why some businesses thrive during uncertainty while others fall apart? By the end of this presentation, you'll have three strategies to navigate change with confidence."*

B. Share a Story

Use a brief anecdote to connect emotionally with your audience:

- *"A year ago, a small team used AI to tackle a problem that had stumped an entire industry. Today, I'll show you what they did—and how you can apply their approach to your own challenges."*

C. Use a Metaphor

Frame your objectives as part of a larger narrative:

- *"Think of this presentation as a journey. Together, we'll make three key stops: identifying the challenge, exploring solutions, and mapping out your next steps."*

D. Highlight the Stakes

Motivate your audience by emphasizing what's at risk:

- *"Every day you delay adapting to digital transformation, your competitors gain ground. Today, I'll equip you with the tools to not just keep pace—but to lead."*

E. Make It Personal

Engage your audience by relating the objectives directly to their experiences:

- *"Raise your hand if you've ever struggled with work-life balance. By the end of this talk, you'll walk away with three actionable strategies to reclaim control."*

F. Preview the Journey

Offer a clear roadmap of what's ahead:

- *"In the next 20 minutes, we'll explore the why, the what, and the how of building a winning strategy."*

G. Share a Surprising Fact

Start with a compelling statistic to grab attention:

- *"Did you know that 70% of change initiatives fail? Today, I'll explain how to make sure you're in the successful 30%."*

H. Connect to a Broader Goal

Tie your objectives to a larger purpose to inspire your audience:

- *"In a world that's changing faster than ever, understanding AI isn't optional—it's essential. My goal today is to show you how to turn AI into a tool for innovation and growth."*

It's More Than a Formality

Introducing objectives is more than a formality—it's your chance to set the stage for a meaningful experience. Whether you simply state your objectives or tie them into your hot opening, the way you frame your goals can captivate your audience and keep them engaged from start to finish.

Now, think about your next presentation. How will you make your objectives not just clear—but unforgettable?

2. **Story**: Stories breathe life into your message. They're not just anecdotes; they're strategic tools that make your presentation relatable and memorable. One story may be all the influence you need. Or you may need to employ multiple stories to help the audience reach the ultimate goal. It all depends on the length of your stories and the duration of your presentation. For each story follow the SPA formula: *Story, Point, Action or Apply*. Start with a compelling narrative, drive it home with a singular point, and end with a **clear call-to-action** or **call-to-application** (CTA).

The 'S' stands for **story**—a narrative of related events, actions, or experiences. Stories captivate your audience's attention and make your presentation more relatable. They serve as powerful tools to illustrate a point or provide context for your topic. These stories can range from personal anecdotes to historical or literary examples.

Every presentation is context-sensitive, so the key is to select stories that align with your message and resonate with your audience. A well-chosen story not only enhances understanding, but also leaves a lasting impression.

Stories are at the heart of Executive Presence, but not just any story will do. Strategic stories are designed with purpose—they go beyond entertainment to persuade, educate, inspire, and leave a lasting impact. These narratives actively shape listeners' beliefs, values, and behaviors, making them more than just a fleeting moment of amusement.

The essence of a strategic story lies in its **point**—the 'P' that ties directly to your objectives. A clear, singular, and meaningful takeaway transforms a story from a pleasant anecdote into a powerful tool. As Joel Schwartzberg suggests in *Get to the Point*,[10] your point should complete the sentence, *"I believe that..."* It must be strong enough to provoke thought, yet specific enough to resonate deeply. Avoid cluttering your story with multiple ideas or overly complex messages; this risks losing clarity and focus. Instead, let your point stand alone, free of conjunctions like "and," to maximize its impact.

A great story doesn't need to spell everything out. Often, the most effective points are implied, allowing the audience to connect the dots through the narrative's details. This approach respects the audience's experiences and perspectives, inviting them to engage and interpret rather than dictating what to think.

---

10. Joel Schwartzberg. Get to the Point! Sharpen Your Message and Make Your Words Matter. United States: Berrett-Koehler Publishers, 2017. Page 9

Also, not every story has to originate in the business world to make an impactful point about it. In fact, some of the most memorable business lessons stem from unexpected places—a chance encounter, a natural phenomenon, or even a childhood memory. These stories tap into universal truths, offering fresh perspectives on leadership, teamwork, resilience, or innovation. They resonate because they connect on an emotional level, transcending industry jargon and creating relatable, human moments that inspire action and reflection.

Take this example, a story I love to share:

From as early as I can remember until I turned 12, my family had dinner at my mother's parent's house every Friday night. I loved seeing my grandparents, but what I remember most about those dinners are my grandmother Rae's potato pancakes.

My grandmother always made the best potato pancakes. They had a nice oval shape; they were never overcooked; never too crunchy; but they were also never too soft or too mushy. They were perfect.

I often find myself wishing I had asked her how she made them, because for more than 40 years now, I have been trying to replicate my grandmother's perfect potato pancakes.

See, as the youngest of her seven grandchildren, I was just a teenager when my grandmother died. It had never occurred to me to ask her for her recipe. By the time I realized I wanted to know it, it was too late. And, to my surprise, my mother didn't have the recipe either; just like me, she never thought to ask for it.

With my grandmother's passing, we not only lost her, but also her treasured recipe, and all her other wisdom and experience.

As a professional speaker, I travel a lot. And that means I dine at a lot of restaurants all over the world. Whenever I spot potato pancakes on the menu, I always order some, hoping to find anything even close to my grandmother's perfect potato pancakes.

I keep searching, but never finding.

In storytelling workshops I've facilitated, I've asked participants to reflect on what the story about my grandmother's potato pancakes could symbolize in a business context. Here's a partial list of responses:

- Document Knowledge
- Transfer of Knowledge is Vital
- Never Assume
- The Value of Uniqueness
- Legacy Matters
- Consistency in Quality
- Preserve Core Values
- Continual Learning & Improvement
- The Danger of Undervaluation
- Treasure Intangible Assets
- Preserving Heritage
- Seize the Moment
- Value of Experience
- Continuity and Connection
- Regret
- The Search for Identity
- Conversations Matter
- The Irreplaceability of Personal Touch

What makes a story impactful in a business context isn't its origin, but its ability to convey a lesson that inspires action or shifts perspective.

Sometimes the connection between the story and its application is obvious, directly reinforcing your message. Other times, the link requires explicit articulation. To clarify your intended takeaway, consider using bridge phrases like *"For me..."*, *"This made me realize that..."* or *"What I learned was..."* By sharing what the story meant to you, you're not telling people what to think—you're giving them something to think about.[11]

These bridge phrases act as signposts, guiding your audience from narrative to meaning. They provide clarity without diminishing the audience's role in drawing conclusions, ensuring your story is not just relatable and memorable, but actionable.

To craft a strategic story, start with the point you want to make. This clarity saves time and ensures your narrative aligns with your objectives. The goal isn't just to be memorable—it's to spark change, inspire action, and leave your audience thinking long after the story ends.

When done well, a strategic story does more than entertain—it becomes the 'because' that connects your ideas to the real world, shaping how people think, feel, and act.

Every person in your audience is carrying two unspoken questions: *Do I want to change?* and *Can I?*

Desire comes first. Without a compelling reason—without that spark—motivation fizzles. You've seen it happen: great ideas, inspiring presentations, ambitious goals—all fading into the background because the *why* wasn't strong enough. But when that spark catches? That's when possibility opens up. That's when we can begin mapping the *how*—the plan, the path, the next steps that turn intention into action.

---

11. I'm inspired by Bernard Cecil Cohen's insight from <u>The Press and Foreign Policy</u>: "The press may not be successful much of the time in telling its readers what to think, but it is stunningly successful in telling its readers what to think about." (Princeton University Press, 1963, p. 13).

Storytelling and influence converge in the 'A' of the SPA formula: a **Call-to-Action (CTA)** or **Call-to-Application**. This is your catalyst for moving an audience—not just inspiring them, but guiding them toward action, reflection, or change. Just as every story needs a clear point, every presentation needs a CTA that lays out the way forward. Maybe it's a shift in perspective. Maybe it's a concrete step—ideally with a timeline to encourage follow-through.

A well-crafted CTA focuses on the listener's needs, not your own. It invites the audience to take what they've just heard and apply it in a meaningful way. Whether it's adopting a new mindset, embracing a feeling, or taking action, a strong CTA ensures your message doesn't end when the presentation does—it lingers, resonates, and creates real-world impact.

That's the difference between a presentation that's merely memorable and one that's truly *moveable*.

3. **Transition**: Think of your ideas as islands and transitions as the bridges connecting them. Without smooth transitions, your presentation risks feeling fragmented and hard to follow. To ensure a seamless flow, combine visual and verbal transitions for maximum impact.

    Visual transitions involve deliberate physical movements or changes in stage positioning to emphasize a shift in focus. For instance, moving to a different spot on stage for each story or point helps your audience mentally organize and retain the information. Importantly, move silently between points, allowing the action itself to signal a change.

    Verbal transitions are equally effective. Phrases like *"Let's dive deeper into this," "Have you ever wondered about...? Well, let's explore it,"* or *"Here's what this means for you"* guide your audience smoothly from one idea to the next. These cues provide clarity and ensure your presentation maintains a natural rhythm.

Combining both: Use movement and words together to create a cohesive transition. As you move from one part of the stage to another, verbalize the shift, letting the action reinforce your message. For example, *"Now that we've tackled X, let's move on to Y,"* with your movement timed to the verb in your statement, it enhances both engagement and retention.

4. **Interaction:** Humans have a remarkably low boredom threshold, and it's shrinking. To keep your audience engaged, follow the 7/20 rule—add a stunning visual or shift their physicality every 7–10 minutes for in-person presentations and every 2–3 minutes for virtual ones. Actively involve them every 20 minutes.

    Interactions can take many forms. For example: asking your audience to raise their hands, jot something down, or nod in agreement. A simple *"Give me a thumbs up,"* or directions like *"Look to your right"* or *"Stand up,"* all qualify as interactions. You can ask a question and offer three possible answers for them to choose from. Pose a controversial question, encourage them to turn to a neighbor and share their thoughts, or take out their phones and respond to a digital poll.

    "Change the medium to break the tedium"

    At its core, an interaction is anything that creates oxygen. Why does this matter? Oxygen is essential for staying alert. Movement increases oxygen levels, keeping your audience awake, engaged, and energized. Interaction also fosters connection and recharges energy levels, helping everyone stay focused on your message.

    And don't forget: take breaks. After all, *"The brain can only absorb what the butt can endure."*[12]

5. **Closing:** If the opening sets the stage, the closing ensures the curtains fall with impact. Restate your objectives, recap key points, and tie your ending back to your beginning. Use a clincher—a powerful quote, a thought-provoking challenge, or a final story—to leave a lasting impression.

---

12. This pithy comment likely originated with Louis Agassiz, a 19th-century scientist. However, its exact origin remains unclear, as it has been widely used in the context of education, speaking, and meetings to emphasize the importance of breaks and audience comfort.

Restating Objectives

Restating your objectives at the conclusion of a presentation is also more than a formality—it's your chance to make your message unforgettable. It's the penultimate brush-stroke on the canvas of your presentation, reinforcing the core purpose and leaving your audience with a sense of clarity and accomplishment.

Why does this matter? Because repetition cements understanding. It ensures your audience remembers the journey they've just been on, and it emphasizes the takeaways they'll carry forward. For longer presentations, it's a lifeline, reminding listeners of what might have faded in the mix of details.

Restating objectives also brings your presentation full circle. It ties your conclusion back to your introduction, creating a sense of cohesion and polish. For persuasive presentations, it's your moment to underscore the actions you want the audience to take, locking in your CTA—**Call-to-Action** or **Call-to-Application**.

More than anything, revisiting your objectives demonstrates value. It shows how your presentation addressed their questions, solved their problems, or opened doors to new possibilities. It's your opportunity to leave a lasting impression and prompt reflection. Did the audience get what they needed? Are they inspired to act? By restating objectives, you invite them to assess their own transformation and provide meaningful feedback.

Creative Ways to Restate Objectives

Just like a strong opening sets the tone, a powerful restatement anchors the conclusion. You could restate your objectives with, *"I met my objectives by...,"* or, you could choose fresher ways to make your objective recap resonate:

A. Weave a Narrative

Transform your objectives into a story, wrapping up the journey you've taken your audience on.

- *"We began by defining the challenge, examined the obstacles in our way, and uncovered actionable solutions. Today, you leave with the tools to adapt, the strategies to grow, and a vision for success. This is your roadmap forward."*

B. Echo a Metaphor

Revisit a metaphor introduced at the start of your presentation to create a full-circle moment.

- *"Remember the bridge we set out to cross? With today's insights, you now have the blueprint, the tools, and the confidence to build your way forward."*

C. Invite Personal Connection

Encourage your audience to see themselves in your objectives.

- *"As we wrap up, ask yourself: How will you apply these strategies to tackle your biggest challenges? What steps will you take to turn these ideas into action?"*

D. Reference a Story

Callback[13] to an opening story or statistic to make your objectives tangible.

- *"Earlier, I told you about a team that revolutionized their approach with three simple steps. Now, you have those same steps to apply in your work, starting today."*

E. Create Rhythm

Use repetition or a punchy structure to drive your message home.

- *"Adapt to lead. Innovate to grow. Stay bold to stay ahead. These are the pillars of your future success."*

---

13. A **callback** is a rhetorical technique where the speaker references something mentioned earlier in the presentation—such as a humorous comment, story, idea, audience input or key point.

Structure

F. **Inspire Possibility**
    Paint a vivid picture of what's achievable.

- *"Imagine a team where collaboration drives innovation, clarity fuels decisions, and resilience ensures growth. With these three strategies, that vision is within your grasp."*

G. **Make it Actionable**
    Offer clear next steps the audience can implement immediately.

- *"We've explored the challenges and identified the solutions. Now, take these three steps: embrace change, empower your team, and prioritize innovation."*

H. **End with Humor**
    Add a light, unexpected twist to make your restatement stick.

- *"So, in the end, success isn't rocket science– it's clarity, confidence, and remembering to hit 'save' on your big ideas."*

I. **Use a Quote**
    Anchor your message with an inspiring quote that ties back to your objectives.

- *"As Maya Angelou said, 'Do the best you can until you know better. Then, when you know better, do better.' Now, you have the steps to know—and do—better."*

J. **Issue a Challenge**
    Conclude with a call to action that sparks momentum.

- *"You have the tools. You have the roadmap. Now, I challenge you: take the first step today. What will you achieve by this time next year?"*

By restating your objectives in a memorable way, you amplify your message and ensure your audience leaves not just informed, but inspired to act. Now, the stage—and the possibilities—are theirs.

Handling Q&A

Ending your presentation with a Question & Answer session can weaken your message, leaving the audience with someone else's question as their final takeaway, rather than your carefully crafted conclusion. Consider integrating questions throughout your presentation to sustain engagement, or address them just before your closing remarks. This approach allows you to address audience concerns while ensuring your final words leave a strong, lasting impression. Always let your voice—and your message—be the last thing they hear.

Crafting the Perfect Exit Line: The Lasting Echo of Your Message

Close your eyes and imagine you're standing on stage having just delivered the best presentation you've ever delivered. The spotlight warm on your face. The audience leaning in, eager to hear your final words. What do you say? How do you ensure the ending resonates, inspires, or provokes reflection long after the applause has died?

An exit line isn't just a conclusion; it's a culmination. It's the moment where your message crystallizes into something that clings to memory, like a melody that plays in the back of the mind. Done right, it transforms your presentation from something heard to something felt—a lasting gift you leave with your audience.

Why the Last Line Matters

Consider this: most people remember the beginning and the end of any experience.[14] In a movie, it's the opening scene and the final frame that linger. In a book, it's the first chapter and the last sentence that stick. Your presentation is no different. While your audience might forget specific details, they'll carry the feeling and impact of your closing words.

---

14. The observation that information presented at the beginning (Primacy) and end (Recency) of a learning episode tends to be retained better than information presented in the middle was first introduced by B. B. Murdock (1962). The serial position effect of free recall. Journal of Experimental Psychology, 64(5), 482–488. https://doi.org/10.1037/h0045106

Structure

John F. Kennedy understood this when he said, *"Ask not what your country can do for you—ask what you can do for your country."* It's rhythmic, resonant, and unforgettable. It's not just a sentence; it's a call to action.

Your exit line should serve a similar purpose. It should align with the theme of your presentation and evoke the emotion you wish to leave behind—whether it's inspiration, motivation, or curiosity.

Crafting an Exit Line That Clings

To create a memorable closing statement, start with these principles:

1. **Pithy:** Keep it short, but full of meaning. Clever and thought-provoking. A strong exit line is like a tweet—compact, but impactful.

2. **Memorable:** Use rhythm, repetition, or rhyme to make it stick. Think about the cadence of Kennedy's or Martin Luther King Jr.'s speeches.

3. **Resonant:** Connect it to the audience's emotions and your core message. What do you want them to feel as they leave? Hope? Determination? Wonder?

4. **Original:** Avoid clichés. Instead, craft something that feels fresh and authentic to your voice.

Here's a simple exercise: ask yourself, *If my audience could only remember one thing from this presentation, what would it be?* Then shape your exit line around that.

Inspiring Examples

Let's break down some potential exit lines for different contexts:

- **Innovation Keynote:** *"The future doesn't wait. Neither should we. Let's build it together."*

- **Leadership Workshop:** *"Great leadership isn't about moments of glory—it's about showing up every day. Show up, lead, repeat."*

- **Install Kick-off:** *"A closed deal isn't the end; it's the beginning of something extraordinary. Let's start today."*

- **Visionary Presentation:** *"The only thing standing between today and the future we imagine is the action we take now."*

Notice the common thread? They're concise, audience-focused, and emotionally charged.

Delivering the Mic Drop

Once you've crafted the perfect line, deliver it with purpose. Slow down, emphasize the key words, and let the silence that follows do its work. If you choose to preface your exit line with, *"I'd like to leave you with this..."* use it sparingly and with confidence.

And most importantly? Stop talking. No last-minute add-ons. No explanations. Trust your exit line to hold its weight.

Closing Thoughts

Your exit line isn't just the end of your presentation—it's the start of your audience's journey with your ideas. So, make it count. Make it memorable. Make it yours.

I'd like to leave you with this: an exit line is a chance to say something unforgettable. Don't waste it.

Modular Approach

This modular approach lets you tailor your presentation for different events by swapping out the middle sections while keeping the opening and closing intact. It also allows you to adjust the length on the fly by adding or removing modules to fit the available time. The brilliance of this method lies in its seamlessness—the audience remains unaware of these adjustments, ensuring your presentation stays impactful and memorable.

> *"In limits, there is freedom. Creativity thrives within structure."*[15]

Cohesion and Clarity

Every story you include must serve a purpose. Before crafting a story, ask yourself: *What's the point I want to make?* Clarity is non-negotiable. Craft a single sentence that encapsulates your presentation's core message and ensure every module supports it. Think of this as your destination, with each module acting as a vehicle to get you there.

Business Presentations: From Portal to Oracle

Business presentations offer a unique challenge: conveying complex information without losing engagement. Too often, presenters fall into the trap of becoming a '**Portal**'—a mere conveyor of data. The goal is to be an '**Oracle**'[16]—a visionary who inspires action.

Emotional Connection

Emotion is the glue that makes ideas stick. Facts may inform, but emotions inspire action. Frame your data within a story of triumph, collaboration, or innovation. Instead of presenting a product's technical specifications, tell the story of how it solved a problem or changed lives. This approach makes your message memorable and your audience invested.

---

15. Julia Cameron, "The Artist's Way for Parents: Raising Creative Children", TarcherPerigee, 2014
16. I believe the admonition to 'Be a Oracle not a Portal' has been conveyed by others, though I could not locate any print references.

Audience-Centric Approach

Your presentation isn't about you; it's about them. Start by understanding your audience's needs, challenges, and motivations. For instance, if you're presenting to retail executives, address their concerns about shifting customer behaviors or supply chain disruptions. By tailoring your content, you're not just delivering a presentation—you're offering solutions.

Structuring for Impact

Every presentation should have a core message supported by **Must-Haves:** the essentials that deliver on your promise to the audience; **Nice-to-Haves:** elements that add depth or richness, but aren't critical; and, **Leave-Behinds:** valuable extras that don't fit within the allotted time, but can be provided as additional resources. This prioritization ensures your message stays focused and impactful. Present multiple perspectives to create a balanced narrative, acknowledging potential drawbacks alongside benefits. This transparency builds trust and credibility.

Refinement Through Feedback

Great presentations are iterative. Seek feedback after every delivery. Did the audience engage? Were they confused by any part? Use these insights to refine your content and delivery.

Avoiding Content Suffocation

Too much information is just as harmful as too little. Content suffocation—or 'Death by PowerPoint' and 'Death by Data'—happens when an audience is overwhelmed with too much information, data, or ideas at once, hindering their ability to absorb and retain key points. Leaving them disengaged.

Simplicity is Key

Think of your slides as billboards: concise headlines, meaningful visuals, and minimal text. Let your spoken words provide the details. Balance data with storytelling to humanize your message and make it relatable.

Structured Clarity

Present your ideas in a logical sequence, such as: problem, solution, benefits. This structure ensures clarity and helps your audience follow along effortlessly. Incorporate moments of engagement, like a quick poll or a thought-provoking question, to keep the energy high.

Engaging the Audience

Engagement isn't just about holding attention—it's about creating a connection. Use physical activities, like asking the audience to stretch or interact with neighbors, to refresh their focus. Leverage technology like AI tools or AR/VR to enhance interactivity and adapt to modern preferences.

Action Steps:

1. **Define Your Destination:** Craft a single, concise sentence that encapsulates your presentation's core message. Use this as your guiding principle to maintain clarity and focus throughout your preparation.

2. **Assemble Modularly for Flexibility:** Organize your presentation into self-contained modules: Opening, including objectives; Stories; Transitions; Interaction; and Closing with an exit line. This modular approach allows you to tailor your presentation for different audiences and time constraints seamlessly.

3. **Transform Data into Emotion:** Select one to three stories that connect emotionally with your audience and align with your key objectives. Use the SPA formula (Story, Point, Action) to ensure your stories inspire action and resonate deeply.

4. **Infuse Interactive Energy:** Plan meaningful interactions every 7–10 minutes for in-person presentations and every 2–3 minutes for virtual ones. Examples include asking questions, conducting quick polls, or inviting small physical activities to maintain engagement and boost oxygen flow.

5. **Design Visual Impact:** Audit your slides to prioritize simplicity: one idea per slide, with a focus on impactful visuals. Balance storytelling with data to humanize complex concepts and maintain your audience's attention.

6. **Elevate Transitions for Flow:** Combine verbal cues with physical movements to signal shifts in focus. For example, use phrases like *"Let's explore this further"* while changing your position on stage, creating seamless connections between your ideas.

7. **Refine and Repeat:** After each delivery, gather feedback from trusted sources or your audience. Look for areas where clarity, engagement, or flow could improve, and iterate for future presentations.

8. **Prepare for Dynamic Q&A:** Integrate audience questions during the presentation to maintain engagement and ensure their final takeaway comes from your crafted closing statement.

9. **Close with Lasting Impact:** Craft a powerful closing statement that echoes your message, ties back to your opening, and leaves a memorable impression. Ensure your final words are succinct, audience-centered, and actionable.

By embracing these principles, you'll move beyond merely delivering content to creating presentations that inspire action, foster connection, and leave lasting impressions.

Chapter Seven

Craft Presentations Like a Pro: How Lessons From a Classic Fable Can Amplify Your Impact

Creating a presentation is like stepping into a fable: deceptively simple at first, but revealing layers of complexity the closer you look. One story, in particular, illustrates this perfectly—the tale of *The Apprentice and the Printer*.

In the story, a seasoned printer and their apprentice examine a freshly printed sheet. The printer, standing back, declares it flawless, content with the overall appearance. The apprentice, however, leans in and spots minor imperfections—misaligned letters, faint smudges—details invisible to the casual observer. While small, these flaws hold the potential to diminish the work's quality.

The Duality of Crafting a Keynote

This fable encapsulates the dual perspectives every presentation demands: the broad overview and the detailed inspection. Both are vital, but they serve different purposes.

- **The Broad Overview:** Ensures your ideas flow, your narrative engages, and your conclusion resonates.
- **The Detailed Inspection:** Reveals gaps in logic, awkward transitions, or missed opportunities for impact.

When I finished the first draft of my latest keynote, it felt complete. But as I revisited it with a critical eye, I began to notice the 'smudges'—gaps in the logic, untapped opportunities, and moments that lacked clarity. With each revision, the keynote became sharper, more cohesive, and ultimately more powerful.

Influence Amplified

The Creative Tension Between Two Perspectives

The balance between these two perspectives is what makes presentation creation both challenging and rewarding.

- The **big picture** keeps your message compelling and aligned with your audience's needs.
- The **details** ensure your delivery is flawless and impactful.

Switching between these modes of thinking can feel dizzying, but it's the iterative process of refining drafts that turns a good keynote into a great one.

Embrace the Process

Awareness is your saving grace. Recognizing that frustration is part of the creative process makes it easier to embrace. Every draft is an opportunity to zoom out for perspective and then zoom in to perfect the details. This dual focus helps you create a presentation that holds up under both scrutiny and admiration.

By draft five, my keynote had evolved into something tighter, clearer, and more impactful than I could have imagined in the first draft. While it still wasn't 'perfect,' it had undergone the necessary transformation to deliver the impact I wanted.

The Lesson of the Fable

The fable of *The Apprentice and the Printer* reminds us that excellence lies in embracing both perspectives. The apprentice's attention to detail and the printer's broad perspective are equally essential. Together, they create a final product that is both polished and profound.

As a presenter, you must embody both roles. Zoom out to ensure your presentation connects with your audience's goals. Zoom in to refine transitions, smooth out inconsistencies, and eliminate distractions. It's a dance between the big picture and the fine details—a dance that produces truly exceptional work.

Action Steps:

1. Begin your presentation development by outlining the 'big picture.' Identify the central message and the journey you want your audience to take.

2. Once your draft is complete, revisit it as the apprentice would—scrutinize transitions, logic, and clarity.

3. Seek feedback from trusted colleagues. They can act as an outside perspective, spotting what you might overlook.

4. Use each revision to tighten your content. Remove redundant points, enhance transitions, and refine anecdotes.

5. Embrace the iterative process. Dedicate time to revisit and refine each draft until your presentation holds up to both the broad overview and detailed inspection.

Chapter Eight

Keep It Fresh: 3 Techniques to Make Every Presentation Relevant and Memorable

Every time you step onto the stage, you have a choice: deliver the same presentation you've given before or adapt to meet the evolving needs of your audience. The best presenters know that keeping a presentation fresh isn't just a strategy—it's a necessity. Audiences change, industries shift, and your topic evolves. To remain relevant and memorable, your approach must evolve, too.

The good news? You don't need to reinvent the wheel. There are three key moments to refresh your presentation: **between presentations**, **between drafts**, and **in the moment**. Let's explore how to make the most of each.

1. Between Presentations: Harnessing Feedback

Every presentation offers a treasure trove of insights—if you're willing to listen.

- **Audience Questions:** During Q&A, the questions people ask reveal what they found unclear, intriguing, or particularly relevant. Treat these as direct feedback on your content's effectiveness.

- **Subtle Reactions:** Pay attention to body language, engagement levels, and energy in the room. Where did people nod along? When did their attention waver?

Incorporate this feedback into your next presentation. By addressing what resonated and refining what didn't, you show your audience that you're not just speaking—you're listening. This iterative process keeps your material fresh and ensures it aligns with your audience's needs.

2. Between Drafts: Evolving with Your Audience

When preparing a presentation, you tailor it to meet your audience's current level of knowledge. But here's the catch: between drafting and delivering, your audience may have evolved.

- Have they gained new insights or experiences?
- Are they grappling with new challenges or opportunities?

If your presentation feels 'stuck in the past,' you risk losing their attention. To stay relevant:

- Update your content to reflect recent developments in your field or industry.
- Dive deeper into topics if your audience has grown more sophisticated.
- Adjust your framing to meet their current priorities and concerns.

Refreshing your drafts ensures your presentation remains timely, dynamic, and impactful.

3. In the Moment: Reading the Room

Even with meticulous preparation, no two audiences are the same. Great presenters excel at the art of adaptation. Observing your audience's reactions to your words enables you to steer the interaction and command the atmosphere — a skill commonly known as 'reading the room.'[17]

- **Gauge Engagement:** Are people leaning in or zoning out?
- **Respond to Cues:** If a particular point sparks interest, expand on it. If a section isn't landing, pivot quickly.

This real-time flexibility transforms a pre-scripted presentation into a meaningful conversation. It shows your audience that you're not just delivering a message—you're connecting with them in the moment.

---

[17]. The concept of understanding or assessing the mood or atmosphere of a situation is universal. In Japanese, the concept is called "Kūki wo Yomu," which literally translates to "reading the air." In Spanish, one might use the phrase "captar la onda" which means "capture the wave." In French, the phrase "prendre la température" is used, translating directly to "take the temperature."

Why Freshness Matters

A stale presentation feels like an old rerun—predictable and uninspired. But a fresh one? It grabs attention, sparks curiosity, and leaves a lasting impact. Refreshing your content shows your audience that you value their time and insights. More importantly, it ensures your message resonates deeply and authentically.

Chapter Wrap-up: Embrace the Evolution

Your presentation is a living document, not a static script. By revisiting and refining your material, you ensure it remains relevant and engaging. Whether you're preparing for your next keynote or adjusting on the fly, remember: the more you adapt, the more you connect.

Action Steps:

1. After each presentation, review audience questions and feedback. Use this to refine your content for future presentations.

2. Before delivering a presentation, reassess your audience's current priorities. Adjust your framing or content as needed.

3. Practice reading the room by delivering your presentation to small groups and observing their reactions.

4. Keep a 'living' file of your presentation, updating it regularly with new insights, data, and stories.

5. Record your presentations and review them critically. Identify moments that could be stronger, clearer, or more engaging.

Chapter Nine

How Tailored Presentations Inspire Action, Build Trust, and Drive Lasting Impact

You might be surprised to learn that every person in the room is looking to you for something deeply personal to them. The spotlight is on you, and in each set of eyes lies an unspoken expectation—not for broad strokes, but for meaning that resonates on a personal level. Meeting that expectation begins with understanding that your presentation isn't about a topic; it's for an audience, tailored to their needs, challenges, and aspirations. It's not about what you want to say, but about what they need to hear, feel, and understand. A great presentation isn't a performance; it's a gift designed specifically for the audience in front of you. When you tailor your message with intention, you move beyond words and create true resonance—the key to inspiring action, shifting perspectives, and turning passive listeners into engaged collaborators.

Understanding Diverse Audiences

Your audience isn't just a group—it's a mosaic of individuals, each with unique priorities and expectations. To truly connect—and ultimately influence—you need to address their personal *'why.'* Consider three examples: C-suite executives, key employees (2ICs), and rank-and-file employees.

- For C-suite leaders, your message should show how it aligns with their long-term vision and addresses their big-picture goals.
- For key employees, speak to the practical, actionable solutions they need to bridge strategy and execution.
- For rank-and-file employees, focus on how your ideas make their work easier and more meaningful.

Your presentation isn't about your expertise—it's about meeting them where they are, addressing their concerns, and delivering the insights they need to take the next step.

To bridge these perspectives, create a narrative that acknowledges each group's priorities. Highlight the big-picture strategy for executives, actionable steps for managers, and tangible benefits for employees. By weaving these elements together, you build a cohesive message that resonates across the spectrum.

Presenting to C-Suite Executives

C-suite executives are visionaries who thrive on clarity and impact. When addressing them, focus on three core elements:

1. **Strategic Alignment**: Demonstrate how your proposal advances the organization's mission and long-term objectives.

2. **Risk vs. Reward**: Provide a balanced analysis of potential outcomes, showing how benefits outweigh risks.

3. **Resource Investment**: Articulate what it will cost in terms of time, money, and effort—and the return on that investment.

Avoid overwhelming them with details. Instead, craft a narrative centered on outcomes and impact, illustrating how your ideas align with their strategic goals.

Engaging Key Employees / 2ICs

Key employees are the operational linchpins. They're the ones who translate strategy into action, so your message must address their priorities:

- **Achieving Goals:** Show how your proposal helps them hit departmental KPIs.

- **Practicality:** Highlight the feasibility of your ideas, ensuring they can be implemented with minimal disruption.

- **Influence on Decision-Making:** Acknowledge their role as advisors to the C-suite and champions of change within the organization.

Position yourself as a partner in their success by providing actionable insights that empower them to bridge strategy and execution.

Relating to Rank-and-File Employees

The rank-and-file employees are the practitioners who will execute your vision. To gain their trust and cooperation, your message must:

- **Simplify Daily Workflows:** Show how your ideas will make their tasks easier and more efficient.
- **Highlight Immediate Benefits:** Focus on tangible improvements, such as time savings or streamlined processes.
- **Address Pain Points:** Demonstrate empathy by directly tackling their challenges.

Connecting with these employees requires practicality and transparency. When they see the value in your message, they'll become your most enthusiastic advocates.

The Power of Customerizing[18] Presentations

Customerizing—or tailoring—your presentation to suit the specific audience is where true connection happens. Tailoring your presentation isn't about changing your message; it's about shaping it to feel personal and relevant. Think of it as creating a conversation with your audience—not talking at them, but speaking for them. Use industry-specific references, relatable anecdotes, and humor that feels authentic to their experiences. Small adjustments, like acknowledging their unique challenges or referencing their industry trends, show that you've put them at the center of your presentation. When you make the message for them, you move from being a presenter to being a partner.

When you customerize, you signal that you've done your homework. This effort builds credibility and fosters trust, setting you apart from presenters who rely on generic content. Even a small adjustment—such as referencing an industry trend or using their terminology—can make your presentation unforgettable.

---

18. A neologism popularized by several authors starting in the early 1990's discussing mass customization of products. Here we are using it to describe customizing a presentation for a specific audience. The term customerization, was also used by Wind, Jerry, and Arvind Rangaswamy in "Customerization: The Next Revolution in Mass Customization." Journal of Interactive Marketing 15, no. 1 (2001): 13–32. https://faculty.wharton.upenn.edu/wp-content/uploads/2012/04/0104_Customerization_The_Next_Revolution_in.pdf.

Building Credibility and Trust

Trust begins with empathy. When your examples mirror their challenges and your solutions align with their realities, your audience recognizes that your message is crafted for them. This thoughtful approach not only builds credibility, but also demonstrates that you're offering genuine value tailored to their world. Personalization transforms you from a presenter into a trusted partner, deeply invested in their success. With this foundation of trust, your influence grows, ensuring your message resonates with greater impact.

Standing Out in the Speaking Industry

In a crowded field, differentiation is everything. Customerized presentations not only engage audiences, but also elevate your reputation. By tailoring 20% of your content to a specific audience while keeping 80% consistent, you deliver a bespoke experience without excessive effort. This balance allows you to stand out and secure repeat bookings.

Achieving Event Goals

Event organizers aren't just looking for a good presentation; they want measurable outcomes. By aligning your presentation with the event's objectives—e.g., inspiring change or sparking innovation—you deliver results that matter. Tailored content resonates deeply, motivating audiences to take action.

Forging Emotional Connections

Emotional resonance transforms a presentation into an experience. By sharing stories that reflect your audience's challenges and triumphs, you make the message for them. These moments of shared understanding show your audience that you see them, hear them, and understand them. It's this connection—not your slides or statistics—that will make your presentation unforgettable.

Adding Value for Event Organizers

Tailored presentations don't just benefit audiences; they enhance the success of the entire event. Higher attendee satisfaction makes organizers look good, increasing your chances of future engagements. Highlight your customization efforts during post-event conversations to showcase your unique value.

Growing Personally and Professionally

Each tailored presentation is an opportunity for growth. Learning about different industries and adapting to diverse audiences expands your expertise and refines your material. Engaging with attendees before and after events provides invaluable feedback, helping you evolve as a presenter.

Boosting Sales and Marketing Potential

Offering customerized presentations gives you a competitive edge. Event organizers value presenters who go the extra mile, leading to referrals, repeat bookings, and a reputation for excellence. Building these relationships transforms one-time engagements into long-term partnerships.

Action Steps:

1. **Research Your Audience**: Use surveys, interviews, or organizer insights to understand audience roles, priorities, and challenges.

2. **Tailor Content Strategically**: Adjust up to 20% of your presentation to include audience-specific examples, language, and humor.

3. **Craft Multi-Layered Messaging**: Address big-picture goals for executives, actionable steps for managers, and tangible benefits for employees.

4. **Engage Actively**: Use polls, activities, or Q&A to create a dialogue and ensure audience involvement.

5. **Evaluate and Improve**: Collect feedback from audiences and organizers to refine your approach for future presentations.

Tailoring your presentation isn't just a strategy; it's a commitment to making your message meaningful, memorable, and actionable. When done well, it transforms a good presentation into a defining moment of connection and impact.

Part Four
Humor and Emotional Connection

What makes a leader not just heard but unforgettable? It's the ability to connect on a deeper level, and one of the most effective tools for building that connection is humor. Now that you have the tools and techniques to structure your presentation, this section explores how levity, laughter, and lightheartedness can elevate Executive Presence and foster trust. Humor isn't about being a comedian—it's about building bonds, breaking down barriers, and making your message resonate.

From understanding the science behind oxytocin, the 'trust hormone,' to refining the art of timing and relevance, these chapters reveal how to use humor strategically. Whether it's easing tension with a touch of levity, weaving in relatable anecdotes, or inspiring trust through shared laughter, you'll uncover actionable strategies to enhance your Executive Presence. Ready to leave a lasting impression? Let's dive into the lighter side of influence.

Chapter Ten

The Humor Bridge: Build Trust and Influence Through Strategic Laughter

Has this ever happened to you: You're sitting in a conference room, anxiously waiting for a high-stakes presentation to begin. The presenter, a senior executive, strides to the front of the room with a commanding presence. But instead of diving into a dry, fact-laden monologue, they open with a self-deprecating anecdote about the time they accidentally sent an email meant for their partner to the entire company. The room erupts in laughter, and just like that, the tension dissolves. What happens next is nothing short of magical—the audience leans in, engaged and open. Why? Because trust has been built, one laugh at a time.

> *"A wonderful thing about true laughter is that it just destroys any kind of system of dividing people."*[19]

At the heart of this phenomenon lies a simple truth: humor is more than entertainment. It's a profound tool for fostering trust, enhancing leadership, and connecting with others on a deeply human level.

> *"When you have laughed with someone… you tend to feel a bond with that person"*[20]

Laughter's Secret Ingredient: Oxytocin

Trust, much like the invisible thread of a spider's web, binds people together in meaningful relationships. But what's the science behind this connection? Enter oxytocin, often dubbed the 'trust hormone.'[21] This remarkable molecule, released during moments of positive social interaction, acts as the glue for human bonds. From a warm handshake to shared laughter, oxytocin primes us to trust and cooperate.

---

19. John Cleese. Interview with Nathan Rabin, tv.avclub.com. February 5, 2008.
20. Claudia E. Cornett, Learning Through Laughter: Humor in the Classroom, Phi Delta Kappa Educational Foundation, 1986, pg. 11
21. Emily A. Holmes, ed., "Storytelling increases oxytocin and positive emotions and decreases cortisol and pain in hospitalized children," PNAS, June 1, 2021, https://www.pnas.org/content/118/22/e2018409118.

The fascinating link between laughter and oxytocin cannot be overstated. When you share a genuine laugh with someone, your body releases this trust-enhancing chemical. It's not just a fleeting moment of joy—it's a biological response that strengthens the bridge between you and your audience. Think of humor as the scaffolding of this bridge, supporting the weight of influence and connection.

The Leadership Superpower: Humor

Leadership is about influence, and influence begins with connection. Humor, when used thoughtfully, is a superpower that makes leaders more relatable and approachable. Picture a CEO addressing a room of skeptical employees during a challenging reorganization. Instead of diving into spreadsheets and jargon, they start with a humorous story about their own first day at the company—when they couldn't find the restroom. Laughter ripples through the audience, breaking down barriers and creating a sense of camaraderie.

Humor isn't about being a stand-up comedian; it's about finding the light in shared experiences. It humanizes leaders, making them more memorable and trustworthy. But as with any tool, humor must be wielded with care. The wrong joke at the wrong time can alienate rather than unite.

Speaking with Impact: Humor's Role on the Stage

Great presenters know that humor is a gateway to the audience's hearts and minds. A well-timed quip or a funny anecdote doesn't just entertain—it primes listeners to absorb your message. Laughter creates a mental reprieve, making complex ideas more palatable.

Consider this: You're delivering a presentation on a technical topic. Instead of launching into jargon, you share a relatable observation about how even smart devices seem to misunderstand you—cue the story of asking your voice assistant for *"news"* and getting *"nudes"* instead. The laughter that follows doesn't just lighten the mood; it opens the door for deeper engagement.

However, humor must always serve the message, not overshadow it. The best humor underscores key points, creating an emotional anchor that helps the audience remember your content long after the applause fades.

The Relatability Factor: Everyday Humor

The most effective humor often springs from life's ordinary moments. Personal anecdotes, quirky observations, and shared challenges resonate because they're genuine. Think of the endless memes about virtual meetings or the universal experience of a coworker accidentally leaving their mic on during a call. These moments connect us, cutting across hierarchies and cultural differences.

Authenticity is crucial. Forced jokes or canned humor can backfire, eroding trust rather than fostering it. Instead, draw from your own experiences. Recall the time you spilled coffee on yourself moments before a critical pitch or the absurdity of a printer breaking down just when you needed it most. These relatable stories do more than entertain—they create bonds, serving as the threads that weave you closer to your audience. So, instead of only focusing on how to add humor to your presentation, look for ways to uncover the humor already within it.

Levity with Intention: Balancing Humor and Seriousness

Humor is a spice, not the main dish. It adds flavor, but too much can overwhelm. In leadership and in presenting, the balance between levity and gravity is crucial. A light-hearted moment can make a heavy topic more approachable, but it should never trivialize the subject.

Consider a presenter addressing a serious issue like workplace burnout. They might open with a humorous observation about the absurd number of emails they receive daily. This levity disarms the audience, creating an atmosphere of trust, before transitioning into actionable strategies for reducing stress.

Testing the Waters: Refining Your Humor

Great humor often looks effortless, but it rarely is. Behind every seemingly spontaneous quip is preparation. Test your material in low-stakes settings, like team meetings or casual conversations. Pay attention to what lands— what is well-received—and what isn't.

Humor requires finesse, especially in professional settings. Avoid sarcasm, controversial topics, or anything that risks alienating your audience. Seek feedback from trusted colleagues to ensure your humor aligns with your message and audience expectations.

> "After the laughter, the learning begins."[22]

Risks and Rewards

Like any powerful tool, humor carries risks. A poorly timed or off-color joke can alienate listeners or undermine credibility. And without credibility, trust cannot exist—these two virtues are inseparable. But when used thoughtfully, humor's rewards far outweigh its risks. It fosters trust, deepens connection, and transforms speakers and leaders into memorable, relatable figures.

Action Steps:

1. Reflect on your daily experiences and jot down moments of levity. Use these as inspiration for future presentations.

2. Practice delivering humor in casual settings to refine your timing and gauge reactions.

3. Incorporate humor that complements, rather than overshadows, your message.

4. Test your material with trusted colleagues to ensure it aligns with your audience and objectives.

5. Balance humor with gravity, using levity to connect without trivializing important topics.

6. Remember that authenticity is key—draw from relatable, personal experiences to forge genuine connections.

---

22. Many authors have expressed a similar idea, though the original source cannot be determined.

Part Five
Leveraging Multi-Sensory Engagement

In your mind's eye can you already picture yourself stepping into a room and holding your audience's attention, not just with words, but with an experience that speaks to all their senses? This section dives into the transformative power of multi-sensory storytelling, a technique that elevates presentations from mere information-sharing to unforgettable journeys.

By blending visuals, sound, touch, taste, and even smell, you can create an immersive environment that captivates and inspires. These chapters explore how to orchestrate your presentations like a skilled conductor, weaving each sensory element into a harmonious narrative that resonates deeply with your audience. Ready to transform your next presentation into a symphony of engagement? Let's continue.

Chapter Eleven

Creating Multi-Sensory Presentations That Captivate and Inspire

Prepare to uncover the secret to crafting a presentation that goes beyond the ordinary—a performance where words come alive, dancing across the stage with expert precision. Welcome to the world of multi-sensory storytelling, where captivating an audience becomes an art form elevated to extraordinary heights.

In this immersive experience, you become the conductor, orchestrating a symphony of sights, sounds, and sensations that leave an indelible mark on your audience's hearts and minds. Gone are the days of monotonous monologues and soulless slides. Instead, you weave a tapestry of visuals, music, and textures that transport your listeners on a journey they'll never forget.

As you take center stage, the lights dim, and every eye is fixed upon you. This is no mere presentation; it's an expert-level exploration of sensory storytelling. Your body language becomes an extension of your words, each gesture a brush stroke on the canvas of your narrative. As you step forward, your audience leans in; as you pause, they hang on the silence. Each member of the audience is captivated by the rhythm of your movements and the cadence of your voice.

Now, let's explore the sensory elements that will elevate your presentations to the stratosphere:

Evoking the Senses

Just as a chef adds spices to elevate a dish, infusing your presentations with sensory experiences creates a memorable journey. By using props, devices, and other media to bring your narrative to life, you engage the senses of sight, sound, taste, touch, and smell. You enrich your story and ignite your audience's imagination, creating a feast for the senses.

Visuals: Curate slides that breathe life into your story, serving as vibrant backdrops for your words. Incorporate captivating images and infographics that amplify your message, transforming each slide into a scene that immerses your audience in your narrative.

Sound: Harness the power of music and ambient sounds to underscore pivotal moments and transport your listeners to different environments. Whether it's a haunting melody that tugs at their heartstrings or the bustling sounds of a city street that transports them to a new world, sound is a potent tool in your storytelling arsenal.

Taste: Creatively incorporate flavors that align with your theme, creating sensory anchors that enhance recall and leave a lasting impression. My favorite is to use Reece's Peanut Butter Cups. They have a distinct taste, and they are a great example of innovation. A handful of candy hearts or a bite of chocolate can become a mnemonic device, forever linking your message to a sweet memory.

Touch: Distribute tactile props or samples, fostering physical engagement and interaction with your content. Whether it's a tangible product sample or a simple stress ball, inviting your audience to interact with your presentation through touch deepens their investment in your story.

Smell: Though challenging, strategically infusing scents can evoke powerful emotional connections and memories. A whiff of freshly baked bread or the subtle aroma of a fragrant flower can transport your audience to a different time and place, forever intertwining your message with their olfactory recollections.

Remember, every element of your presentation should work in harmony, like the instruments of a well-tuned orchestra. You are not merely sharing information; you are creating an experience that will resonate long after you've taken your final bow. This is your concert, and every note, every brush stroke, every texture, and every aroma matters.

So, take charge, captivate your audience, and let your presentation sing. Embrace the power of multi-sensory storytelling, and watch your words come alive, leaving a lasting impact on the hearts and minds of your audience. Without these elements, your presentation risks being monotonous. Remember to always add zest!

Action Steps:

1. Use vibrant, high-quality images, infographics, and minimal text to enhance your message.

2. Select background music or sound effects that underscore your presentation's emotional beats or thematic elements.

3. Use edible props or flavors that tie into your presentation theme as sensory anchors.

4. Provide tactile props or items that align with your story or message.

5. Incorporate scents that enhance your story and leave a memorable impression.

6. Ensure all sensory elements—visuals, sounds, touch, taste, and smell—work together harmoniously.

7. Practice your presentation multiple times, incorporating each sensory element to ensure timing, harmony, and flow.

8. Test your multi-sensory presentation with a small group to gauge its impact.

Part Six
Story crafting

Reflecting on what we've covered so far, Part One laid the groundwork by examining the traits that define exceptional leaders—confidence, authenticity, and composure. In Part Two, we explored storytelling as a powerful tool to inspire, connect, and simplify complex ideas. Part Three guided us through structuring presentations that captivate, resonate, and leave a lasting impression. In Part Four, we uncovered how humor can build trust, foster connection, and make your message unforgettable. Finally, Part Five introduced the art of engaging all the senses to create truly immersive experiences.

In this section, you'll uncover how to harness the timeless power of storytelling to elevate your communication and forge deeper connections with your audience. Strategic storytelling sits at the crossroads of art and science, weaving together ancient wisdom and modern insights to craft narratives that captivate, inspire, and transform. Since life seldom presents us with neatly packaged stories complete with simple conflicts and well-defined characters, it's your responsibility to shape these raw moments into cohesive and compelling narratives. What makes a story unforgettable? Is it the vivid imagery that lingers, the emotional resonance that moves, or the clarity of its message?

From uncovering the emotional core of a story to balancing logic with creativity, these chapters will guide you through the art and nuance of crafting narratives that truly resonate. You'll learn how to transform dry data into compelling tales, leverage pivotal moments to amplify your message, and uncover the extraordinary stories hidden in the fabric of everyday life.

Influence Amplified

Whether you're commanding a stage or leading a boardroom discussion, storytelling is your bridge—linking ideas to action, emotions to intellect, and people to purpose. By the end of this journey, you won't just understand the mechanics of great storytelling; you'll embrace your potential to craft stories that leave a lasting impact.

Chapter Twelve

Storytelling: The Bridge to Connection and Persuasion

"Form follows function."[23]

Imagine standing before a towering bridge, its intricate design both awe-inspiring and functional. Beneath it flows a powerful river, dividing two worlds—emotion and logic. As storytellers, our mission is to construct bridges that span this divide, connecting hearts and minds with purpose and precision. These bridges are built not of steel and stone, but of stories, each carefully crafted to transport, transform, and persuade.

The Power of Purpose in Storytelling

Every story begins with a purpose, just as every bridge begins with a destination in mind. Purpose-driven storytelling isn't merely a technique; it is the foundation upon which meaningful narratives are built. Consider the story of an architect designing a building. Their purpose dictates every choice—the shape of the structure, the materials used, and even its location. Storytelling works the same way.

When we tell stories, purpose guides the narrative form. A tale of innovation may call for a clear, concise structure to emphasize breakthroughs and milestones. Conversely, a story about community thrives in rich, descriptive detail, evoking a tapestry of shared experiences. Without purpose, a story becomes aimless, like a bridge that leads nowhere.

---

23. This is the more often used version of what Louis Sullivan wrote in his 1896 essay, *The Tall Office Building Artistically Considered.* The actual words are, "It is the pervading law of all things organic and inorganic, of all things physical and metaphysical, of all things human and all things superhuman, of all true manifestations of the head, of the heart, of the soul, that the life is recognizable in its expression, that form ever follows function. This is the law."

Think about the last story that captivated you. Was it the intricate plot, the vivid characters, or the poignant message? Likely, it was all of these—but each element was shaped by the story's core purpose. As storytellers, our role is to discern this purpose and let it guide the narrative's flow, ensuring authenticity and engagement. This approach avoids the pitfalls of generic storytelling, where form feels forced and content suffocates.

Purposeful storytelling isn't just about sharing experiences—it's about influencing change. Whether you're inspiring a team, pitching an idea, or sharing a personal journey, every story should be crafted with a clear goal in mind. What do you want your audience to think, feel, or do differently? And what specific behavior shifts are essential to making the desired change happen? When you start with that clarity, your story becomes more than just words—it becomes a catalyst. When purpose shapes the narrative, your stories resonate more deeply, shaping decisions and influencing actions in ways that create real, lasting impact.

Crafting Stories That Open Hearts and Wallets

Now, picture yourself embarking on a journey—not just any journey, but one that delves into the rich tapestry of human experience. As Peter Guber eloquently puts it in his seminal work, *Tell to Win*, "We are in the emotional transportation business."[24][25]

This is the heart of storytelling: the art of moving people emotionally. Stories are far more than vehicles for information—they are transformative vessels, capable of stirring hearts, inspiring action, and leaving a lasting impact. Guber's insight is simple yet profound: to truly connect with others and influence their decisions, you must engage both their emotions and their rational minds—their heads and their hearts.

Storytelling bridges the gap between emotion and logic, forging connections that persuade, inspire, and resonate deeply. It's the ultimate tool for creating meaningful influence, blending the power of feeling with the precision of thought.

---

24. Peter Guber, Tell to Win (New York: Crown Business, 2011). Pg. 25.
25. https://www.verywellmind.com/what-is-narrative-transportation-5217042

Human decisions are rarely made in the cold, rational light of reason alone. Neuroscience reveals a powerful truth: emotion sparks decisions, while logic justifies them.[26] Think of a moment when you felt compelled to act—to buy something, to support a cause, or to embrace a new idea. Was it the data alone that convinced you, or was it the story behind the numbers that truly moved you?

Effective storytelling intertwines emotion and logic, leading the audience on a journey. Begin with struggle and challenge, capturing the emotional core of your narrative. Then, guide your listeners to resolution, weaving in facts and data to reinforce the outcome. When your audience feels emotionally invested in the story's resolution, they align themselves with your vision.

> *"The head won't go where the heart hasn't been"*[27]

Techniques for Engaging and Transformative Stories

How do we craft stories that inspire action? The answer lies in balance—harmonizing the emotional and intellectual dimensions of storytelling. To succeed, we must embrace both art and science, empathy and evidence. Consider these techniques:

- Paint vivid pictures with your words. Describe sights, sounds, and feelings to immerse your audience fully in the narrative.
- Use relatable analogies to make complex ideas accessible, transforming abstract concepts into tangible experiences.
- Share authentic stories drawn from personal experiences or the lives of your audience. Authenticity builds trust and connection.

A well-told story is more than a series of events; it is a carefully curated experience. Engage all senses, evoke emotions, and lead your audience on a journey where the outcome feels not only desirable, but inevitable.

---

26. See: Antonio R. Damasio. <u>Descartes' Error: Emotion, Reason, and the Human Brain</u>. New York: Penguin Books, 1994. Kahneman, Daniel. Thinking, Fast and Slow. New York: Farrar, Straus and Giroux, 2011. Zaltman, Gerald. <u>How Customers Think: Essential Insights into the Mind of the Market.</u> Boston: Harvard Business Review Press, 2003.
27. The specific source of the phrase is unknown.

Putting Stories into Action

Storytelling isn't just an art; it's a discipline that requires practice and reflection. As you stand at the threshold of influence, remember this: your power lies not just in the stories you tell, but in the emotional journeys you create. You are not merely a storyteller; you are an architect of transformation. Your mission is to inspire, your currency is connection, and your tool is the timeless craft of storytelling.

Action Steps:

1. **Identify the Purpose**: Reflect on your story's core goal. What do you want your audience to think, feel, or do differently? Let this purpose guide your narrative.

2. **Engage Emotionally**: Begin with the heart. Identify the emotions you want to evoke and craft your story to resonate with these feelings.

3. **Balance Emotion and Logic**: While emotion draws the audience in, logical reasoning solidifies their support. Use facts to enhance, not replace, the emotional connection.

4. **Create a Relatable Journey**: Structure your story with a clear beginning (struggle), middle (challenge), and end (resolution). Ensure the journey is relatable and inspiring.

5. **Practice Authenticity**: Share stories that feel genuine, drawn from personal experience or the audience's reality. Authenticity fosters trust.

6. **Use Relatable Analogies**: Make complex ideas accessible with metaphors and analogies that connect to familiar experiences.

7. **Test and Refine**: Share your story with a trusted colleague or mentor. Seek feedback on its emotional impact and clarity.

Let your stories transform ideas into action, bridging the gap between what is and what could be. By embracing the power of purpose and emotional connection, you'll craft narratives that not only captivate, but also compel. So, where will your story lead today?

Chapter Thirteen

Turn Your Life Lessons Into Universal Stories That Resonate

"When you're speaking in the truest, most intimate voice about your life, you are speaking with the universal voice." Cheryl Strayed[28]

There are moments in every life where the ordinary meets the profound. Maybe it was the time you stood at a crossroads, a single decision shaping the course of your future. Or perhaps it was a fleeting exchange—a smile, a word, a gesture—that altered how you saw the world. These moments, though personal, hold the potential to connect deeply with others. They are the seeds of stories that transcend the individual, weaving universal lessons from personal threads.

Ancient Wisdom: Pathos, Ethos, Logos

The art of storytelling has ancient roots. The Greeks, renowned orators and philosophers, understood its power and distilled it into three essential elements: Pathos, Ethos, and Logos. Together, they form a triad that has guided narratives for centuries.

Pathos appeals to emotion. It's the reason your heart aches when the hero falters or soars when they triumph. Imagine a tale where a farmer, battling drought and despair, finally sees rain on the horizon. It's the tug at your heartstrings that makes the story unforgettable.

Ethos is credibility, the anchor that makes you trust the storyteller. Picture a mentor sharing hard-earned wisdom or a researcher citing discoveries. Their authority makes the narrative not just compelling, but believable.

---

28. Cheryl Strayed is an American author known for her memoir, *Wild*. As quoted by Maria Popova in the newsletter the Marginalian (formerly Brain Pickins), June 15, 2015, emphasizing the profound connection between personal authenticity and universal resonance in storytelling. https://www.themarginalian.org/2015/06/15/cheryl-strayed-longform-podcast-interview/

Logos is the logic, the structure underpinning the narrative. It's the roadmap that ensures every twist and turn leads somewhere meaningful. Without Logos, even the most emotional or credible stories can lose their way.

But wait, as they say on late-night TV. There's more! Timing is everything in storytelling. The ancient Greeks called it **Kairos**—the art of seizing the perfect moment. It's not just about crafting a powerful message; it's about delivering it when your audience is most ready to hear it. Kairos is what turns a good story into an unforgettable one, ensuring it resonates emotionally, culturally, and situationally. It's the subtle difference between a story that inspires and one that fades into the background.

Kairos works on multiple levels. A story rooted in cultural relevance taps into the moment's zeitgeist, meeting your audience where they are and amplifying your message. It's the story that feels like it was made for the times. The audience's emotional readiness is just as crucial. A hopeful tale shared after a setback can lift spirits, while a cautionary one during turbulent change can provide clarity. Then there's situational context—tailoring the narrative to a specific meeting, a shifting industry, or even a personal milestone. Stories told at the right time can hit with laser-like precision.

Even within the narrative, timing shapes impact. Reveal a pivotal twist too early, and the tension evaporates. Drag out the resolution, and you risk losing your audience's attention. Effective storytelling is about pacing—building momentum, delivering impact, and leaving your audience with a lasting impression.

Imagine a leadership retreat. Share an inspirational story on day one, and it might set a pleasant tone. But wait until the group has wrestled with challenges and feels fatigue creeping in—that's when your story becomes unforgettable. That's when Kairos transforms words into a shared, meaningful experience.

When these elements align, they craft a story that resonates deeply—emotionally, intellectually, and credibly. The harmony of Logos, Pathos, Ethos, and Kairos ensures your story isn't merely heard, but profoundly felt. It's the key to storytelling that doesn't just capture attention, but leaves a lasting impression, delivering the right message at precisely the right moment.

Modern Insights: Perceptive, Cognitive, Affective

Fast forward to today, where neuroscience sheds new light on storytelling. It introduces us to another trio: Perceptive, Cognitive, and Affective elements. These components delve deeper into how stories engage our brains.

Perceptive elements bring stories to life through sensory details. You're not just told about the rain; you hear it patter against the roof, smell the damp earth, and feel the cool droplets on your skin. Such vividness anchors the audience in the narrative, making it tangible.

Cognitive elements engage the mind, presenting facts and frameworks. In the farmer's story, this might mean understanding the science of drought-resistant crops or the economic impact of agriculture. These details add depth, grounding the story in reality.

Affective elements stir emotions, much like Pathos. They tap into joy, sorrow, fear, and hope, ensuring the audience doesn't just process the story, but feels it.

Together, these elements transform stories into multi-dimensional experiences. They don't just inform; they immerse, inspire, and linger long after the last word.

Building Bridges: The Convergence of Frameworks

What happens when ancient wisdom meets modern science? Magic. By balancing Pathos, Ethos, and Logos with Perceptive, Cognitive, and Affective elements, storytellers craft narratives that are as engaging as they are impactful.

Consider a story about a young entrepreneur navigating a volatile market. Pathos connects us to their fears and dreams. Ethos ensures we trust their journey. Logos structures the narrative, guiding us through challenges and triumphs. Meanwhile, Perceptive details paint the bustling market, Cognitive elements reveal economic data, and Affective moments share the entrepreneur's elation and despair. This balance creates a story that resonates universally, blending personal experience with broader lessons.

The Role of Imagination: Creative License

Here's another secret: your stories don't have to be strictly factual to be true. Emotional truth often outweighs factual precision. You're telling a story, not giving a deposition. Think of the movies that have moved you. Were every detail and character perfectly accurate, or did the story's core ring true?

Using creative license isn't about deception; it's about enhancement. You might combine several real-life events into one or exaggerate a detail for emphasis. Perhaps in the entrepreneur's tale, you imagine the market as chaotic and vibrant, even if you've only seen pictures. These creative choices bring the story to life, making its lessons more vivid and memorable.

Transforming Facts into Feelings

Facts are important, but they rarely stand alone. To connect, they need context and emotion. Storytelling turns dry data into something relatable. For example, instead of stating, *"50% of small businesses fail within five years,"* tell the story of one business owner's journey—their struggles, their resilience, their lessons. The statistic remains, but now it's felt.

Emotional Truth: The Heart of Storytelling

At its core, storytelling is about authenticity. It's not about recounting every detail exactly as it happened, but about capturing the essence of the experience. This emotional truth allows your audience to see themselves in your story. They feel the entrepreneur's fears because they've faced their own. They celebrate the triumph because they, too, know the taste of hard-earned success.

When your story invites the audience to participate—to feel, reflect, and act—it transforms from personal anecdote to universal lesson.

Action Steps:

1. **Blend Elements Thoughtfully with Timeliness**:
   Combine Pathos, Ethos, Logos, and Perceptive, Cognitive, and Affective elements, ensuring the story aligns with the audience's emotional and situational readiness. Reflect on *when* your audience is most open to your message—whether it's during a moment of change, challenge, or celebration.

2. **Anchor in Emotional Truth at the Right Moment**:
   Focus on the core emotion or lesson of the story, but also consider when to share it. An inspirational tale might have the most impact after the audience has faced a setback, while a cautionary one may resonate during a time of uncertainty. Timing amplifies the emotional connection.

3. **Engage the Senses in a Way That Resonates Now**:
   Use vivid, sensory details to ground your story in the present or to transport the audience to a moment that mirrors their current reality. Describe scenarios that feel relevant and timely, creating a connection between the story's world and their own.

4. **Simplify Complex Ideas with Timely Relevance**:
   Break down intricate concepts, but tie them to the present context. For example, if discussing innovation, align your story with current industry trends or challenges your audience is facing now. This makes the narrative both relatable and urgent.

5. **Practice Imagination with Situational Awareness**:
   Use creative license to enhance your story, but keep it culturally and situationally relevant. A story that resonates with today's zeitgeist will feel more immediate and impactful than one disconnected from the current moment.

6. **Test for Resonance and Timing**:
   Share your stories with small groups to test their emotional, intellectual, and cultural impact, and refine based on feedback. Pay attention to *when* in a conversation or presentation the story feels most effective, and adapt your timing accordingly.

Your personal experiences are a treasure trove of lessons waiting to be shared. By crafting them into stories that balance emotion, logic, and imagination, you turn moments into messages that connect deeply and resonate universally.

Chapter Fourteen

Emotional Arc and Depth in Business Storytelling

You're standing before a room filled with executives. The stakes couldn't be higher. The data on the screen behind you is clear and compelling, yet the room feels disconnected. You notice shifting eyes, the telltale signs of disengagement. Then, you pause. Instead of continuing with facts, you begin to tell a story—one about a small business owner who risked everything for a dream, faced near-certain failure, and ultimately triumphed. As the story unfolds, the energy in the room shifts. You see it in the audience's eyes: you have their attention.

This is the power of storytelling. When it connects at a human level, it transforms passive listeners into engaged participants. But crafting such stories requires more than recounting events. It demands emotional depth and a clear emotional arc.[29]

Emotional Depth: The Heartbeat of Storytelling

Imagine a story that begins with a character standing in a storm. Wind howls, rain lashes, and lightning illuminates the chaos. But what grips you isn't the storm itself; it's the way the character's hands tremble as they clutch a photograph, their tears mixing with the rain, and the fire in their eyes as they take a determined step forward. This is emotional depth—the ability to make your audience not just see, but feel.

In business storytelling, emotional depth isn't optional; it's essential. A story that conveys both external action and internal struggle connects on a profound level. It bridges the gap between abstract ideas and human experience, making your message resonate long after the presentation ends.

---

29. A literary and narrative device used to describe the rise and fall of tension, conflict, and resolution within a story.

Crafting Clear Emotional Arcs

An emotional arc is more than a sequence of events; it's the rise and fall of feelings that guides your audience through a transformative narrative. The purpose of a story is to transport the audience emotionally, ideally through a range of emotions. If your story is only humorous, you're limiting your audience to a single emotional experience. But if you can make them laugh before they cry—or vice versa—each emotion will feel more intense.

Start by introducing lightness or hope, build tension by presenting a challenge or struggle, and resolve it with satisfaction or revelation. For example, share how a company faced an insurmountable challenge, wrestled with doubt, and emerged stronger through innovation. Each phase—challenge, struggle, and triumph—keeps your audience invested and emotionally engaged.

The key to a powerful emotional arc lies in contrast. Juxtapose moments of despair with hope, fear with relief, and failure with triumph. By elevating your audience from one emotional extreme to another, the impact becomes unforgettable. There's a strong connection between how your audience feels at the end of a story and how influential that story is. The stronger the emotions at the conclusion—and the bigger the shift in emotions from beginning to end—the more powerful and resonant your story will be.

A well-crafted emotional arc doesn't just tell a story; it creates an experience. It pulls the audience into the narrative and leaves them with feelings they'll carry long after the story ends.

Show, Don't Tell

Great storytelling immerses the audience. Rather than stating, *"The team was nervous about the project's outcome,"* describe their reactions: *"Their hands fidgeted with pens, voices wavered as they spoke, and the tension in the room was palpable."* When you show emotions through vivid details, you invite the audience to experience the moment themselves.

This principle applies not only to individuals, but to concepts. Instead of declaring, *"The product launch was a success,"* bring it to life: *"As the first orders rolled in, the sound of celebration echoed through the office, and the team's excitement was electric."* Sensory details bring abstract outcomes into sharp focus.

Universal Themes and Relatability

Stories that resonate deeply often tap into universal themes—love, loss, resilience, triumph. These are the threads of shared human experience that bind us all. In business storytelling, weave themes that mirror your audience's reality.

Consider a merger. Instead of focusing solely on financial metrics, frame the narrative as a tale of transformation and adaptability. Highlight the courage to embrace change and the triumph of collaboration. When your audience sees themselves in the story, they're no longer just listeners; they're participants.

The Power of Contrast

Contrast is a storyteller's secret weapon. By juxtaposing opposing elements, you heighten their impact. Imagine describing a CEO's journey from failure to success. Instead of a flat narrative, paint the darkest moments vividly: sleepless nights, rejected pitches, mounting debt. Then, contrast them with the eventual breakthrough—the phone call that changed everything, the team's celebratory cheers. This interplay creates emotional peaks and valleys that keep your audience engaged.

Cultivating Empathy with Relatable Characters

Empathy is the bridge between storyteller and audience. To cultivate it, your characters must feel real. Show their struggles, insecurities, and triumphs authentically. For example, if you're telling the story of a project manager leading a critical initiative, reveal their doubts, the sleepless nights, and the moment they rallied their team. When your audience sees themselves in the characters, the story becomes personal.

Guiding Emotions Through Pacing

Pacing controls how your audience experiences the story. A slow build-up can heighten tension, while a sudden twist jolts them into surprise. Use pauses strategically. After sharing a climactic moment, let silence linger, giving the audience time to absorb the weight of what they've heard. This rhythm mirrors the natural flow of emotions, creating a seamless journey.

Vivid Descriptions and Sensory Details

Words are your palette; use them to paint a picture. Instead of saying, *"The factory was old,"* describe *"Rusted machinery loomed in dim light, the air thick with the scent of oil and damp concrete."* Such details create a vivid mental image, drawing your audience into the scene. Engage multiple senses to add layers of depth—the creak of a floorboard, the sharp tang of fresh paint, or the warmth of sunlight filtering through a window.

Metaphors and Similes: Making the Abstract Tangible

Metaphors and similes translate complex ideas into relatable imagery. For instance, describing a company's restructuring as *"a ship navigating stormy seas"* conveys both challenge and determination. Comparisons like *"Fear gripped the team like a cold hand on their shoulders"* make emotions tangible, enhancing their impact.

Building Multidimensional Narratives

A compelling story operates on multiple levels. It's not just about what happened, but how it felt, looked, and unfolded. Layer your narrative with color, texture, and emotion. For example, a product's development isn't just a timeline of milestones; it's a tale of innovation, setbacks, collaboration, and breakthroughs.

Resonance and Lasting Impressions

The most powerful stories leave a mark. They resonate because they tap into universal truths and shared emotions. As you conclude your story, aim for a note that lingers—a twist, an insight, or a call to action. Leave your audience not just informed, but inspired.

Action Steps:

1. **Map Your Emotional Arc:** Outline the rise and fall of emotions in your story. Identify moments of tension, resolution, and transformation.

2. **Show, Don't Tell:** Use sensory details and vivid descriptions to bring emotions and events to life.

3. **Leverage Universal Themes:** Root your story in experiences your audience can relate to, such as resilience or collaboration.

4. **Juxtapose for Impact:** Highlight contrasts to amplify emotional highs and lows.

5. **Develop Relatable Characters:** Ensure your characters feel authentic and human.

6. **Test for Resonance:** Share your story with a trusted audience. Refine based on their emotional responses.

7. **Conclude with Purpose:** End with a lasting takeaway, call to action, or insight that inspires reflection.

By expertly shaping emotional arcs and depth, you're not just telling a story—you're crafting an experience that lingers with your audience long after the presentation ends.

Chapter Fifteen

Discover the Storyteller Within: How Life's Tiny Moments Engage Your Audience

Storytelling is a profound tool for forging connections, inspiring change, and embedding messages deep within the hearts and minds of your audience. But becoming an exceptional storyteller doesn't start with the telling; it begins with recognizing and collecting stories. This process—blending intuition, observation, and empathy—allows you to uncover the relatable, tiny moments that resonate far more than grandiose, distant narratives.

Before weaving tales that captivate and move, you must first become a story recognizer and collector. Think of this as akin to a chef gathering ingredients before cooking. Having a reservoir of stories at your disposal lets you select the perfect narrative for any occasion without the stress of scrambling under pressure.

The essence of storytelling isn't in recounting epic sagas. It's in finding the extraordinary within the ordinary. Few of us have scaled mountains or survived near-death experiences, but all of us navigate the complexities of daily life. We find joy, sorrow, and humor in the simplest interactions. These moments, when shared, connect us on a fundamental human level.

Cultivating Your Storytelling Practices

To hone your ability to spot stories in everyday life, consider these practices:

Establish Your Own Story Portfolio

Like a chef's pantry, your portfolio of stories should be prepared in advance. Regularly engage in storytelling, even casually, and note which stories resonate with your audience. Catalog these anecdotes, categorize them, and reflect on their contexts or underlying messages. This ensures you're always equipped with a diverse array of narratives.

Keep a Story Journal

Dedicate a journal to your narrative discoveries. Write down stories as they occur or as you recall them. This habit not only solidifies your collection, but also serves as a reservoir of inspiration. Regularly review your journal to uncover connections between different tales or refine existing ones, enriching your storytelling repertoire.

Observe and Reflect

Pay close attention to the details of everyday life. The conversations you overhear, the interactions you witness, and even mundane routines are fertile grounds for storytelling. Look for emotional undercurrents, the unusual within the usual, and personal significance in these moments. Your own experiences—filled with challenges, successes, and lessons learned—offer compelling narratives when tied to universal themes.

Embrace the Mundane and Emotional

Ordinary experiences often yield the most relatable and engaging stories. Emotional moments—whether joyful, surprising, sad, or nostalgic—create powerful foundations for memorable narratives. Observing interpersonal dynamics or listening to conversations can reveal deeper truths about human connections and relationships, offering rich material for your stories.

Capture Sensory Details and Personal Reactions

Vivid descriptions that appeal to the senses can transform a simple moment into an immersive experience for your audience. Reflect on your personal reactions to events or observations. Why do certain moments feel meaningful to you? This introspection adds authenticity and depth to your stories.

Embracing Everyday Moments

By cultivating these habits, you'll become adept at recognizing the small, everyday moments ripe for storytelling. The key lies not in seeking out dramatic events, but in uncovering the extraordinary within the ordinary. Your personal stories, once recognized and collected, can be crafted into presentations and messages that engage, inspire, and move your audience.

Story Crafting

Embrace your daily experiences as stories waiting to be told. By jotting down story prompts and organizing your collection, you ensure your tales feel conversational, relatable, and natural. This preparation eliminates the stress of finding the perfect story under pressure, allowing you to speak with confidence and authenticity. The art of storytelling begins with an open heart, keen observation, and the empathy to find the profound in the prosaic.

Action Steps:

1. **Build a Story Portfolio:** Begin cataloging your stories today. Categorize them by theme or message to create a ready-to-use collection for any occasion.

2. **Start a Story Journal:** Write down moments as they happen or as you recall them. Reflect on their emotional impact and potential narrative use.

3. **Observe Your World:** Take note of the small details in everyday life. Focus on conversations, interactions, and routines that evoke emotions or reveal universal truths.

4. **Find the Extraordinary in the Ordinary:** Reflect on why certain moments resonate with you. How do they connect to broader, shared human experiences?

5. **Practice Vivid Descriptions:** Challenge yourself to use sensory details when recounting events. Describe sights, sounds, smells, and textures to immerse your audience.

6. **Test Your Stories:** Share your stories with trusted friends or colleagues. Pay attention to their reactions and refine your narratives accordingly.

7. **Develop Emotional Awareness:** Identify the emotions tied to your experiences. Use these emotions to guide your audience's connection to your story.

8. **Revisit and Refine:** Periodically review your story journal. Look for new connections and opportunities to enhance your narratives.

Chapter Sixteen

Leverage Critical Moments to Create Compelling Narratives

In business, we often find ourselves in a tug-of-war between different forces. Storytelling is one of those forces—a powerful tool for connection and persuasion—but it's often overshadowed by data and reports. For professionals steeped in expertise, personal stories can feel out of reach, more like a trek up Mount Everest than a practical tool.

I see this frequently in Executive Presence workshops and storytelling coaching sessions. Many executives believe they don't have compelling stories to share because they haven't completed marathons, climbed mountains, or overcome life-threatening challenges. Instead, they rely heavily on data-rich presentations and miss the transformative power of storytelling.

But here's the truth: buried within all those facts and statistics is one person facing a small, but critical moment: a moment of transformation, realization, or revelation that fundamentally alters their world. Sociologist Anthony Giddens calls them "*fateful moments*"[30]—times when events converge, placing a person at a crossroads. These moments, charged with emotion and meaning, are the cornerstone of impactful storytelling.

The Critical Moment: The Heart of a Story

At its core, every captivating story revolves around something interesting happening to one person a critical moment. This moment of transformation, realization, or revelation fundamentally alters the central character's world. It delves into the heart of the human experience—growth, a shift in values, or a profound change in understanding.

---

30. Anthony Giddens. Modernity and self-identity: self and society in the late modern age. United Kingdom: Stanford University Press, 1991. Page 113.

Influence Amplified

The transformation is often internal, such as a change in perspective or belief, but it can also manifest externally in decisions or actions. Audiences connect with these moments because they mirror the challenges, decisions, and revelations we all face.

The critical moment acts as the story's climax, providing depth and emotional resonance. Consider these examples:

- **"The Wizard of Oz" (1939):** Dorothy realizes her heart's desire is to return home to Kansas.
- **"The Seven Samurai"[31] (1954):** Kambei Shimada, the samurai leader, understands that the villagers are the true winners, having secured their future at the expense of the samurai.
- **"Jaws" (1975):** Chief Brody realizes the magnitude of the challenge as the shark attacks Quint's boat, the Orca.
- **"Star Wars: A New Hope" (1977):** Luke Skywalker's decision to trust the Force and turn off his targeting computer during the Death Star assault.
- **Personal Stories:** My grandmother's potato pancakes—the critical moment was realizing her recipe was lost forever. *(see page 46)*
- **Boardroom Example:** During a merger meeting, CEO Steve Mercer realizes the decision isn't just about profits, but touches the company's ethics, leading to the merger's cancellation.

Notice how, in each example, the critical moment happens near the story's end, anchoring the narrative in emotional and transformative power.

Finding and Building Your Critical Moment

What the Story Is About: Great stories don't hinge on monumental achievements or grand adventures. Instead, they focus on a small, pivotal moment—a realization, a decision, or an insight that changes the central character's trajectory. These moments often come with challenges that test the character's resolve, beliefs, and values, heightening the story's stakes and emotional depth.

---

31. I consider The Seven Samurai to be the best movie ever made, directed by the best director, Akira Kurosawa, and staring the world's greatest actor, Toshiro Mifune. The film offers a brilliant showcase of filmmaking and storytelling.

The storyteller's job is to distill the narrative down to this defining moment. It doesn't need to be the biggest event; it just needs to be the most pivotal.

Who, When, and Where: The story's central character is the person experiencing the transformation. The critical moment is when this transformation occurs, often shaped by the setting or context.

Finding the Critical Moment: The critical moment is the pivot around which your story revolves. Without it, the story lacks tension and engagement. If you haven't identified this moment, keep searching. It's the challenge, decision, or realization that changes everything.

Where to Begin: Start your story as close to the critical moment as possible, presenting the 'old normal' before the transformation. This sets the stage for the change to come.

When to End: End your story shortly after the critical moment. Resolve the key conflicts, tie up loose ends, and illustrate the 'new normal.' The greater the emotional distance between the beginning and the end, the more powerful the story's impact.

Crafting Business Stories That Captivate

Business stories don't need to feature grand achievements or death-defying acts. Instead, they focus on relatable, yet critical moments—a decision in a boardroom, a breakthrough during a project, or an unexpected insight during a routine interaction. These moments highlight lessons about leadership, adaptability, and decision-making.

These stories resonate because they reflect universal truths and shared experiences. By focusing on the critical moment, you create a story that inspires and teaches, showing your audience how to navigate their own challenges.

Action Steps:

1. **Identify a Critical Moment:** Reflect on your experiences to find a moment of transformation, decision, or realization. This will be the heart of your story.

2. **Focus on Relatable Events:** Choose moments that mirror common challenges or decisions, making them relatable to your audience.

3. **Build the Emotional Arc:** Highlight the stakes and challenges leading to the critical moment. Show how they shape the protagonist's transformation.

4. **Start Close to the End:** Begin your story as near to the critical moment as possible while providing enough context to set the stage.

5. **End with Resolution:** Conclude shortly after the critical moment, illustrating the new normal or lessons learned.

6. **Use Emotional Depth:** Incorporate sensory details and character reactions to immerse your audience in the story.

7. **Test Your Story:** Share your story with trusted peers. Gather feedback on its emotional resonance and clarity.

Chapter Seventeen

The Power of One: Strategic Stories Are About One Person

Have you ever noticed how the most unforgettable stories are never about crowds or committees? Instead, they focus on one individual—a single person whose experiences resonate far beyond their own life. Stories like these have the power to transform abstract ideas into emotional connections, and they're the foundation of strategic storytelling.

Let's face it, numbers don't move people. You can cite statistics about injustice or innovation all day long, but unless those numbers come alive through a human face, they remain cold and distant. A well-told story about one relatable person doesn't just capture attention; it creates empathy, drawing your audience into a shared emotional journey.

The Proxy Effect: Why One Person Represents Many

When you talk about Rosa Parks, you're not just telling the story of a woman on a bus in 1955. Her courage represents an entire movement for civil rights, and her refusal to move transcends a single act of defiance. The same goes for Anne Frank, whose diary became the voice of millions silenced by the Holocaust. These stories focus on one person, yet their reach and impact are limitless. Why? Because we see ourselves in them.

Authors Chip and Dan Heath explain that audiences connect best when they can relate to and feel for a specific person.[32] People don't naturally connect with ideas, products, or even organizations—they connect with people. It's the personal story that makes the abstract relatable and the unimaginable real.

---

32. Chip Heath & Dan Heath, Made to Stick: Why Some Ideas Survive and Others Die (New York: Random House, 2007) pp. 165-167

More Than a Story—It's a Transformation

Great stories don't just recount what happened. They show transformation. They reveal how the protagonist faced challenges, adapted, and ultimately changed. Think of Steve Jobs starting Apple in a garage and transforming it into a global powerhouse. His journey wasn't just about building computers; it was about innovation, persistence, and vision.

Even a solitary activist like Greta Thunberg turns her individual journey into a rallying cry for global action. She started with a one-person protest, yet her story became a metaphor for youth activism worldwide. This is the magic of strategic storytelling—beginning with one and scaling to many.

Using the Power of One in Business

In business, your audience isn't buying a product; they're buying into a story. The story of how your solution helped an individual overcome a challenge, save time, or find success. Take Erin Brockovich, for example. Her legal fight wasn't just about toxic waste; it was about the power of one person standing up for what's right. That's what audiences connect with.

When crafting your story, identify the 'hero'—the person whose experience represents the larger narrative. Maybe it's a customer who used your product to solve a problem or an employee who exemplifies your company's values. Show their struggle, their growth, and their success. Then, let your audience see themselves in that journey.

Making Stories Actionable

When you finish telling a story, you have the audience's attention, but that's not enough. You want them to feel something, remember it, and act on it. The transition from story to strategy happens when you connect the hero's journey to the broader picture. As Paul Brodeur put it, *"Statistics are human beings with the tears wiped off."*[33] The reverse is also true: human stories add emotion to the numbers.

---

33. Paul Brodeur. <u>Outrageous misconduct: the asbestos industry on trial</u>. New York: Pantheon Books, 1985. 355

Action Steps:

1. **Identify Your Hero**: Find the one person whose journey best illustrates the broader message you want to convey.

2. **Focus on Transformation**: Highlight how they changed through the experience. Growth and challenge make a story compelling. Without change, even microscopic, there is no story.

3. **Bridge the Personal and the Universal**: Show how their story reflects the challenges or aspirations of a larger group.

4. **Simplify the Message**: Keep the story clear and relatable. Avoid unnecessary details that could distract from the core narrative.

5. **Call to Action**: Conclude by inviting your audience to connect emotionally or take a specific next step based on the story.

When you refine the art of strategic storytelling by focusing on one person, you'll unlock the secret to connecting, inspiring, and driving action. So, whose story will you tell today?

Chapter Eighteen

When Numbers Numb: The Art of Data Storytelling

How often has this happened to you: you're sitting in a crowded room, eagerly awaiting a presenter who promises insight and intrigue. Then the slides begin. Numbers—dozens of them—descend like an avalanche: percentages, ratios, projections. Slowly, your focus fades. Your eyes glaze over. The lively chatter in your mind is replaced by an overwhelming urge to escape. What happened? You weren't engaged; you were drowned in data.

The irony is almost poetic. The word "numbers" shares a root with "numb." It's as if language itself is warning us: mishandle data, and you'll lull your audience into a stupor. Yet we persist—hoping that more graphs, bigger charts, and higher percentages will somehow inspire. Spoiler alert: they won't.

Not long ago, I attended a conference on one of my favorite hobbies—fireworks. I was excited to learn from the sessions, but that excitement fizzled out fast. Each presenter had the same approach: PowerPoint slides crammed with endless data. Rows of tiny text and charts overlapping charts. It was like trying to read an encyclopedia through a keyhole.

I lasted a few minutes in each session before heading for the door. It wasn't that their content lacked value; it probably held immense value. But my brain was suffocating under the weight of all that information. The slides weren't sparking curiosity; they were smothering it. I needed space to think, to breathe, to absorb.

When it comes to presentations, even the most dazzling content won't resonate if your audience feels overwhelmed. Just like fireworks need a clear sky to captivate, your message needs room to shine.

Shifting from Raw Numbers to Rich Narratives

The Problem with Pure Data

Data, while powerful, is inherently impersonal. A statistic might explain *what* is happening, but it rarely conveys *why* it matters. Consider this fact: *"42% of employees feel disengaged at work."* Informative? Sure. Memorable? Not without context. Now imagine reframing it: *"Almost half of your team could be silently clocking out before noon."* Suddenly, the number isn't just information—it's a story that hits home.

Let Numbers Paint, Not Overwhelm

Picture a painter. They don't pour every shade of paint onto the canvas at once. They choose colors intentionally, layering and blending to create meaning. Numbers work the same way. Share only what's essential and let each figure serve a purpose. Too much data distracts; the right amount illuminates.

Sprinkle your statistics like morning dew, not a torrential downpour. Instead of presenting ten charts, show one and explain its implications. When your audience feels clarity rather than confusion, they'll be more inclined to follow your story.

When the Board Chair called me in to coach his executive team on presentations, he didn't mince words. "Their presentations suck!" he declared. Naturally, I was curious to see for myself.

The executives, however, thought their presentations were just fine. So, I asked for a demo. The first slide appeared: a wall of tiny numbers crammed into a high-density spreadsheet. It was the kind of slide that could make even an accountant's head spin. The executive dove in, passionately narrating every detail. After two minutes, I had to stop him. "If I can't follow this, what chance does your audience have?"

What started as a one-day engagement turned into two. The team found so much value in rethinking their approach that they asked me to stay another day. Sometimes, the biggest breakthroughs start with the smallest realization: it's not about the numbers—it's about the story they tell.

Every Number Tells a Story

Numbers are far from lifeless. They hold stories of triumph, failure, and transformation. Your role as a presenter isn't to recite numbers; it's to reveal what the numbers mean. For example, instead of saying, *"Our company's revenue grew by 15% last year,"* try: *"Thanks to innovative ideas from teams like yours, we've seen a 15% revenue jump—our highest in five years!"*

This approach gives data a heartbeat. It's no longer just a figure; it's an achievement connected to human effort and possibility.

Engaging Your Audience

Ask, Don't Overload

No one enjoys being lectured to, especially when it involves endless rows of spreadsheets. The secret to engagement lies in interaction. Ask questions. Use visuals. Share relatable examples that bridge the gap between data and human experience.

For instance, if you're discussing market trends, involve your audience: *"Have you have noticed this shift in your own work?"* When people feel like participants rather than spectators, they'll lean in and stay engaged.

Avoid the Danger of Content Suffocation

When preparing a data-heavy presentation, it's tempting to include everything—just in case. But remember: too much data isn't just ineffective; it's counterproductive. An overwhelmed audience retains less, not more. The brain needs time to process, reflect, and connect the dots.

Prioritize quality over quantity. Think of your presentation as a meal: the data is your seasoning, not the main dish. Used sparingly, it enhances. Overused, it spoils.

From Data to Dance

The magic of data storytelling lies in its ability to connect. Numbers alone can't spark emotion or action. But when you weave them into a story, they become memorable. They inspire.

Imagine data as choreography and your narrative as the music. Together, they create a performance that captivates, informs, and resonates. When you become accomplished at this art, your audience won't just listen—they'll remember.

Chapter Wrap-up

Next time you're preparing to present, ask yourself: Do I want to inform or inspire? Data can do the former, but only stories can achieve the latter. Numbers don't have to numb. With a little care, they can ignite curiosity, illuminate ideas, and leave a lasting impression.

So, go ahead—make your data dance.

Action Steps:

1. **Reframe Statistics as Stories:** Take raw data and connect it to human experiences. Make it relatable and memorable.

2. **Simplify Your Visuals:** Use one clear chart or graph per idea. Explain its implications rather than overwhelming your audience with cluttered visuals.

3. **Limit Your Data Points:** Choose only the most essential statistics to support your message. Less is often more.

4. **Add Context:** Provide background and examples that illustrate why your data matters. Turn abstract numbers into concrete stories.

5. **Engage Your Audience:** Ask questions and encourage participation. Make your presentation interactive.

6. **Practice the Balance:** Use data to support your narrative, not dominate it. Think of numbers as highlights in your story, not the story itself.

7. **Test Your Presentation:** Share it with a colleague or friend. Gauge their reaction to ensure your data feels meaningful and not overwhelming.

Chapter Nineteen

The Myth of Short Attention Spans: It's Not Your Audience, It's Your Content

Maybe you can relate: you're at a dinner party, and someone starts telling a story about their day. Ten seconds in, you're already tuning out. Why? It's not because you can't focus—it's because their story is dull, aimless, and doesn't seem to have a point. Now imagine another guest takes the floor, weaving a tale so vivid, funny, or heartfelt that everyone leans in, forks frozen mid-air. The difference isn't your attention span—it's their ability to capture it.

The myth of short attention spans is everywhere. We hear it in marketing meetings, educational seminars, and casual conversations: *"People can't focus anymore."* But here's the truth: it's not that attention spans are shrinking. It's that our tolerance for uninspired, unengaging content has evaporated. We have a low threshold for boredom.

Attention Isn't Dead, It's Selective

Think about the last time you binged a TV series or stayed up late finishing a gripping novel. Your focus didn't waver for hours because the content hooked you. It's the same with audiences. Attention isn't a finite resource—it's elastic, stretching or snapping depending on the content and the deliverer's ability to hold it.

The internet may be full of distractions, but it's also full of proof that people can and will invest their time and focus when something truly resonates. A TED Talk with an enthralling story, a podcast unpacking complex ideas in relatable ways, or a workshop that feels interactive and personal—these all defy the myth of short attention spans.

So, if people are tuning out, the problem isn't their ability to focus. It's what they're being asked to focus on.

The Problem with Blaming Your Audience

When we blame short attention spans, we're really dodging responsibility. It's easier to point fingers at audiences than to reflect on whether the story we're telling is worth their time. But here's the hard truth: as communicators, it's our job to earn attention, not demand it.

Blaming attention spans is like a chef blaming diners for not finishing a bland meal. The solution isn't to shrink the portions; it's to improve the recipe.

The Secret to Captivating Content: Empathy

The best storytellers know that capturing attention—and influencing action—starts with empathy. They don't just think about what they want to say; they think about what the audience needs to hear and how they want to feel.

Are you presenting to busy executives? Respect their time by making your points crisp, clear, and actionable. Presenting to a room of creatives? Infuse your delivery with visuals, metaphors, and an emotional spark. The key is meeting people where they are and crafting an experience that feels tailored to them.

Engagement Over Information

One of the biggest mistakes communicators make is confusing information with engagement. Simply delivering facts or instructions isn't enough—you need to connect. How? By making your audience care.

Start with a compelling hook—a hot opening. (*see page 143*) Share a relatable anecdote, pose a provocative question, or set up a mystery that your content will solve. Keep their interest by weaving in vivid examples, humor, or a surprising twist. And don't just tell; show. Use metaphors, stories, and visuals to make abstract ideas tangible.

Finally, close with purpose. Leave them with a memorable takeaway, an actionable insight, or a question that lingers long after the conversation ends. We discuss this in more detail in Chapter Twenty-six.

The Power of Flexible Storytelling

If you 'read the room' *(discussed on page 66)* and sense your audience's attention drifting, don't panic—pivot. Great communicators are like jazz musicians, improvising based on the energy in the room. If a slide isn't landing, skip it. If your audience leans into a particular question, go deeper. Recognizing when to adapt is just as important as preparing in the first place.

By staying flexible and attuned to your audience's needs, you show them that their engagement matters. And when people feel valued, they reciprocate with their focus.

The Real Challenge

The myth of short attention spans isn't a challenge for audiences—it's a challenge for presenters. It's a call to refine our craft, to approach storytelling with empathy, creativity, and intentionality.

So, the next time you catch yourself thinking, *"People just don't pay attention anymore,"* ask yourself this instead: *"Am I offering them something worth paying attention to?"*

Because here's the secret: attention spans aren't short—they're selective. Your audience's focus isn't a given; it's a gift. Earn it, and you'll discover just how long they can stay with you.

Closing Thought

Attention is a mirror, reflecting the quality of what's in front of it. If it feels like your audience is looking away, don't blame them—reimagine your reflection. Craft stories that captivate, engage, and inspire. After all, when the content resonates, attention follows.

Action Steps:

1. **Start with Empathy:** Think about your audience's needs, challenges, and expectations. Craft your content to resonate with their experiences.

2. **Create a Compelling Hook:** Use an anecdote, question, or surprising fact to immediately capture interest.

3. **Engage with Purpose:** Don't just deliver information. Use stories, visuals, and relatable examples to make your content memorable.

4. **Stay Flexible:** Be ready to adapt your delivery based on your audience's reactions and energy.

5. **Avoid Overloading:** Keep your content focused and concise. Prioritize quality over quantity.

6. **Close with Impact:** Leave your audience with a clear takeaway, actionable insight, or thought-provoking question.

Chapter Twenty

Storytelling Like a Pro: Borrow Hollywood Techniques to Transform Your Impact

Years ago, when I worked in the film industry, Daniel Arijon's book *Grammar of the Film Language*[34] was my guide. It skillfully explains the visual techniques and principles filmmakers use to craft captivating stories. Arijon dives deep into shot composition, camera movements, editing, sound, and lighting, showing how these elements merge to create coherent and engaging visual narratives.

The same narrative techniques that captivate TV and movie audiences can elevate your strategic business storytelling. Here's how:

1. Point of View

Arijon emphasizes choosing the right perspective, much like selecting a camera angle in film. In business storytelling, the perspective—whether from the company's, customer's, or stakeholder's viewpoint—greatly influences emotional connection and understanding.

- **Objective POV / Third-Person Omniscient:** Like a documentary, this perspective provides an impartial overview, useful for presenting factual information, industry data, or market trends.

- **Subjective POV / First-Person Perspective:** This fosters empathy and emotional connection, similar to a character-driven film. Personal anecdotes or testimonials resonate deeply with audiences.

- **Limited POV / Focused Perspective:** Restricting the view to a specific product, service, or department creates intimacy and engagement, akin to a suspenseful character narrative.

- **Multiple POVs / Ensemble Narrative:** Weaving together different perspectives offers a comprehensive understanding, much like an ensemble film.

---

34. Arijon, Daniel. Grammar of the Film Language. United Kingdom: Focal Press, 1976.

- **Shifting POV / Dynamic Perspective:** Transitioning between viewpoints maintains engagement and provides a well-rounded understanding of the business narrative.

2. Shot Composition

In film, shot composition directs attention and provides clarity. Similarly, the focus in storytelling, like shot sizes, can guide your audience's understanding:

- **Establishing Shots:** Set the stage by introducing the company, mission, and context.
- **Wide Shot / Broad Focus:** Provides an overview of the company or industry landscape.
- **Medium Shot / Focused Narrative:** Zeroes in on a specific product, service, or customer segment.
- **Close-Up / Granular Details:** Delve into specific details, case studies, or testimonials to create a deeper emotional connection.
- **Extreme Close-Up / Laser Focus:** Highlight particular features or unique selling propositions.
- **Shifting Focus / Varied Shot Sizes:** Alternating between broad overviews, focused segments, and granular details maintains engagement.

3. Camera Movements

Dynamic camera movements reveal new information, keeping film audiences engaged. In business storytelling, vary your presentation style through anecdotes, data visualization, and interactive elements to sustain attention.

4. Editing

Effective film editing ensures a seamless narrative flow. Similarly, in business, structure your story logically and cohesively. Start strong, progress clearly, and conclude powerfully. Great storytellers are curators, including only the most impactful examples to propel the narrative. As the great filmmaker Alfred Hitchcock said, *"What is drama, but life with the dull bits cut out?"*[35]

---

[35]. Hitchcock said this to François Truffaut in his 1967 documentary Hitchcock/Truffaut.

5. Lighting and Sound

In film, lighting and sound evoke specific emotions and set the tone. In business storytelling, the choice of words, tempo, volume, and pauses can achieve similar effects. Use vivid, descriptive language and strategic delivery to create the desired emotional resonance.

6. Pacing and Rhythm

Just as filmmakers craft the rhythm and pacing of a story through editing, business storytellers should vary their tempo and intensity. Use pauses to punctuate key points and maintain audience engagement.

7. Showing vs. Telling

Great storytellers understand the power of showing, not telling. Use visual elements, vivid language, concrete examples, and personal stories to bring your narrative to life—much like filmmakers rely on visuals and actions.

By adapting these filmmaking techniques, you can craft engaging, emotionally resonant narratives that capture attention and convey messages with clarity and impact. Great business stories, like great films, inspire audiences to feel, remember, and act.

Action Steps:

1. **Choose Your Point of View:** Decide whether your story will be told from the company's perspective, the customer's, or another viewpoint. Align this choice with your audience's needs.

2. **Craft Your 'Shots':** Plan your narrative like a film—start with an 'establishing shot' for context, then zoom into specific details or testimonials.

3. **Incorporate Movement:** Keep your audience engaged by varying your storytelling style—use anecdotes, visuals, and interactive elements.

4. **Edit Ruthlessly:** Remove unnecessary details. Focus on the most compelling moments that drive your message forward.

5. **Set the Tone:** Use your delivery's rhythm, volume, and language to evoke the right emotions.

6. **Balance Pacing:** Alternate between high-energy moments and deliberate pauses to emphasize key points.

7. **Show, Don't Just Tell:** Use metaphors, case studies, and descriptive language to make your message tangible and memorable.

Chapter Twenty-one

What Sings from the Page May Feel Like a Drag on the Stage

You've put in days of work to prepare your presentation. Each story is carefully thought out, and every word is chosen for its strong effect. Your grammar is flawless—the kind that would make your high school English teacher proud. You deliver your presentation with a strong and heartfelt voice. But despite all these efforts, it just doesn't click with your audience. Why?

The answer lies in the difference between words written for the page and words crafted for the stage.

The Common Mistake

A frequent misstep is writing out your presentation and memorizing it word for word. While memorization has its own pitfalls, the real challenge often begins with how the presentation is written. Writing designed for silent reading and writing designed for speaking aloud are vastly different forms of communication.

Stories meant to be spoken use language designed for the ears and the mind. Spoken language thrives on short, punchy sentences, simple words, and active verbs. It mirrors everyday conversation, incorporating repetition and a fluid flow that resonates with listeners. It isn't just about the words themselves; the magic lies in the delivery. The rhythm, pauses, and tone breathe life into the story.

On the other hand, written language is tailored for the eye. It often has a more complex, static structure, filled with details and nuances that invite readers to linger. Readers can reread a sentence or pause to reflect, luxuries an audience listening to a presentation doesn't have.

The Challenges of Spoken Stories

Listeners don't have the ability to revisit previous sentences or anticipate what's coming next. Every line must be clear and immediate, or the audience may miss the next point while processing what they just heard. This is why stories designed for speaking tend to simplify ideas and rely on tangible, relatable language.

What captivates on the page can drag on the stage. Written words are static; they rely on the reader's interpretation to convey their enchantment. Spoken words are dynamic, brought to life by the storyteller's voice, energy, and connection with the audience.

Crafting Stories for the Stage

The difference between spoken and written language means it is best to avoid writing your stories word for word and then memorizing them. Doing so risks making your stories feel dull or confusing.

As the famous writer and aviator Antoine de Saint-Exupéry once said, *"A designer knows he has achieved perfection not when there is nothing left to add, but when there is nothing left to take away."*[36] The same principle applies to storytelling. Stripping away unnecessary elements reveals the core of your story.

Here's how to develop stories that sing from the stage:

1. **Speak First, Write Later** Begin by speaking your story aloud several times. Use a smartphone or computer to record your second or third telling. Don't overthink it; let the words flow naturally.

2. **Refine Through Listening** Listen to your recording and reflect on how it feels. Where did you stumble? Which parts felt too long or didn't connect emotionally?

---

36 Antoine de Saint-Exupery, Wind, Sand and Starts (Boston: Houghton Mifflin Harcourt, 1992) p. 44.

3. **Edit with Precision** Transcribe your story and focus on making it concise. Aim to tell the same story in half as many words. Remove weak or unnecessary phrases and combine minor characters or events where possible.

4. **Enhance for Impact** Add spoken language elements that bring color, texture, and emotional depth. Infuse your story with words and phrases that feel natural to say aloud and invite your audience to connect.

5. **Rehearse and Adapt** Practice your story out loud multiple times. Pay attention to the rhythm and flow. Adjust as needed to ensure it feels conversational and engaging.

Why It Matters

Stories meant to be spoken and stories meant to be read have distinct styles. They differ in structure, detail, language, and the way they connect with their audience. By focusing on crafting stories for the ear, you ensure your words resonate deeply, captivating listeners and leaving a lasting impression.

When you prioritize the art of spoken storytelling, your stories won't just inform or entertain. They'll come alive, connecting with your audience in ways the written word alone cannot.

Action Steps:

1. **Record First:** Speak your story aloud before writing it down. Focus on how it feels to say, not just how it reads on paper.

2. **Transcribe and Trim:** Transcribe your recording and remove unnecessary words or details. Aim for simplicity and clarity.

3. **Infuse Spoken Language:** Add conversational elements like repetition, relatable metaphors, and natural phrasing to make your story engaging.

4. **Rehearse Regularly:** Practice your story out loud, paying attention to rhythm, pauses, and energy. Adjust based on feedback or your own observations.

5. **Test with an Audience:** Share your story with a trusted friend or colleague to gauge its impact. Refine based on their reactions.

Chapter Twenty-two

Beyond the Notes: How Music's Storytellers Can Elevate Your Next Presentation

When you step onto a stage, two possibilities unfold: your words will either captivate the audience or push them away. This is where storytelling becomes your most powerful tool, transforming ordinary presentations into memorable journeys. Intriguingly, the music industry, with its profound storytellers, unfolds as an unexpected mentor, teaching us how to infuse our stories with the kind of depth and color that resonates deeply and draws listeners in. Through their art, musicians show us the path to breathing life into presentations, turning them into vivid, unforgettable experiences.

Crafting the Flow

Think about your presentation's structure like a song. It should move smoothly from one section to the next, building up, peaking, and resolving. This flow keeps your audience hooked, eager to hear what comes next. Just as a great song takes listeners on a journey, a well-structured presentation guides your audience through a narrative arc,[37] delivering moments of tension, clarity, and resolution.

Authenticity: The Heart of the Story

The real power of a story, whether in a song or a presentation, lies in its authenticity. Take Taylor Swift, for example. She connects deeply with her audience by sharing personal experiences through her music. Her vulnerability fosters trust and relatability. In the same way, when we share genuine stories, we create a bond with our audience, making our message resonate on a deeper level.

---

37. A narrative arc is the structured journey a story follows from beginning to end.

The Rhythm of Engagement

Musicians often play with sentence lengths to keep their listeners engaged. Short, punchy phrases hit hard, while longer, descriptive ones pull listeners into a vivid narrative. This balance of rhythm can transform your presentation. Start with a powerful hook, dive into detailed storytelling, and punctuate key moments with impactful statements that linger in the air.

Metaphors and Similes: Making Ideas Tangible

Metaphors and similes—hallmarks of great songwriting—make complex feelings and ideas approachable. These tools transform the abstract into something concrete and relatable. For instance, instead of saying, *"This change is challenging,"* try, *"Navigating this change feels like steering a ship through a storm—daunting, but manageable with the right tools."*

Learning from Music's Storytellers

To inspire your storytelling, here are artists renowned for their narrative brilliance:

1. **Taylor Swift:** Known for detailed storytelling, Swift draws from personal experiences to make her music relatable. Her song "All Too Well" vividly portrays a breakup, showcasing her knack for emotional narrative.

2. **Kendrick Lamar:** Tackling themes like racial inequality and personal struggle, Lamar's "Sing About Me, I'm Dying Of Thirst" intertwines personal and communal stories to create an emotionally rich narrative.

3. **Brandi Carlile:** Exploring love, loss, and humanity, Carlile's "The Story" highlights her ability to connect deeply with audiences through heartfelt storytelling.

4. **The Decemberists:** Renowned for literary lyrics, their song "Leslie Anne Levine" crafts intricate stories that draw listeners into a rich, narrative world.

5. **Sufjan Stevens:** Blending personal anecdotes with broader themes, Stevens' "Death With Dignity" tackles grief and reconciliation with delicate narrative skill.

6. **Hozier:** Combining poetic lyrics with soulful melodies, Hozier's "From Eden" weaves themes of innocence and sin into a complex and relatable narrative.

7. **J. Cole:** Reflecting on fame, poverty, and racial inequality, Cole's "4 Your Eyez Only" delivers a powerful narrative that resonates deeply.

8. **Florence & The Machine:** Ethereal music meets rich storytelling in "South London Forever," which transports listeners through Florence Welch's vivid descriptions of her experiences.

Adopting Storytelling Techniques

These artists exemplify the art of storytelling in music, providing a wealth of narrative techniques that can elevate your presentations. Here's how you can adapt their approaches:

- **Structure your presentation like a song:** Introduce themes, build tension, and deliver a satisfying resolution.
- **Be authentic:** Share genuine stories that reflect your experiences or those of your audience.
- **Play with rhythm:** Use varied sentence lengths to create a dynamic flow.
- **Incorporate metaphors:** Make abstract ideas tangible and relatable.
- **Draw inspiration:** Study music's great storytellers to see how they weave emotion, narrative, and purpose into their work.

By integrating these storytelling methods, your presentations can become memorable experiences that inspire, motivate, and educate. Just like a powerful song, they'll leave a lasting impression on your audience.

Action Steps:

1. **Analyze Your Structure:** Plan your presentation like a song. Ensure it has an engaging introduction, a compelling middle, and a satisfying conclusion.

2. **Be Genuine:** Share personal anecdotes or stories that reflect your values and connect with your audience on a human level.

3. **Experiment with Rhythm:** Mix short, impactful sentences with longer, descriptive ones to keep your audience's attention.

4. **Use Metaphors:** Turn abstract ideas into concrete visuals with relatable metaphors and similes.

5. **Learn from Musicians:** Study the storytelling techniques of your favorite artists. Identify how they evoke emotion and structure their narratives.

6. **Test Your Flow:** Rehearse your presentation to ensure it flows naturally and engages your audience from start to finish.

Chapter Twenty-three

Challenging the 'Know, Like, and Trust' Model for Presenters

The 'Know, Like, and Trust' (KLT) model suggests that people are more likely to buy from, follow, or be influenced by individuals or businesses they know, have a positive emotional connection with, and trust. It's a popular formula, and it makes sense—on the surface. But is it universally effective? As a speaker or executive delivering presentations, relying solely on this approach could actually limit your impact. Let's explore why it's time to rethink this model.

1. Immediate Impact Over Familiarity

When you attend a presentation, do you need to know the presenter to be moved by their message? Not really. Often, the message itself is what resonates, not the person delivering it. It's about content that connects, meets a need, or provokes thought. A compelling idea can make a strong impression, even when it's from someone you've never heard of.

The takeaway? First impressions count. As a presenter, you might only have one opportunity to connect, so make it count. Content that's relevant, powerful, and well-delivered can outshine any lack of familiarity. It's less about being known and more about being compelling right from the start.

2. Respect Over Likeability

The KLT model emphasizes likeability, but should it? Audiences don't necessarily need to like the presenter to respect their expertise. In fact, some of the most memorable moments come from presenters who challenge their listeners, push them out of their comfort zones, and encourage them to rethink what they know.

Authority and expertise command respect, often more than likeability. Thought leaders who aren't afraid to challenge the status quo don't rely on being liked. They create impact because they're confident, credible, and willing to disrupt complacency.

3. Trust Through Value, Not Familiarity

Trust doesn't always come from familiarity. Sometimes, it's built in the moment when a presenter delivers actionable insights and valuable content. An audience can quickly trust a presenter if they perceive the information as useful and reliable.

This type of trust is transactional; it's not about forming a long-term connection. It's about proving value in the time you have. If your message offers immediate solutions or answers a pressing question, trust is established without any prior rapport.

4. Novelty and Disruption Capture Attention

People are naturally drawn to the unexpected. Presenters who offer novel ideas or disruptive concepts have an edge. Audiences are intrigued by fresh perspectives, sometimes even more than by familiar names.

Standing out can be an advantage. A presenter who defies norms or offers an unconventional viewpoint is more memorable. This curiosity often leads to further engagement, regardless of any pre-existing relationship with the audience.

5. Emotional Resonance Over Personal Connection

The KLT model assumes personal connection is essential. But it's not always about building a relationship; it's about tapping into universal emotions and themes. Powerful storytelling can evoke deep emotions, even when the audience doesn't know the presenter.

Focusing on universal experiences—like resilience, change, or triumph—can create a bond without relying on familiarity. The story itself, if told well, is what forges the connection. It's less about rapport and more about the emotional relevance of the content.

6. Message Over Messenger

Audiences prioritize value over the messenger. They want to know what's in it for them, not necessarily who is delivering the information. If you solve a problem, offer insight, or provide a new perspective, you become valuable—whether or not you are liked.

By focusing on the audience's needs, you shift the spotlight from yourself. The content's value outweighs the need for a traditional KLT approach. Audiences care more about the message when time is limited.

7. Borrowed Credibility and Authority

In today's digital age, social proof is influential. Testimonials, endorsements, or associations with reputable organizations can lend credibility. A presenter doesn't need to cultivate KLT personally if a trusted figure introduces them or they are affiliated with a respected brand.

Authority bias is powerful—people often defer to perceived experts. Credentials, titles, and demonstrated expertise can quickly establish authority, bypassing the need for familiarity or likeability.

8. Efficiency in an Immediate Gratification World

Presenters don't always have the luxury of time to build KLT traditionally, especially in brief engagements. Sometimes, there's only one opportunity to capture attention. The focus must be on delivering value immediately.

Adapt to these circumstances by presenting impactful content swiftly and clearly. There's no time for a gradual KLT build-up when attention is scarce and time is short.

9. Relevance Over Relationship

Addressing timely issues or emerging trends often engages audiences more than relying on a relationship. Audiences care more about how relevant the content is to their lives and challenges than knowing the presenter personally.

Customerization is essential. *(see page 71)* Tailoring your presentation to your audience's needs or interests shows understanding and relevance, which can make up for a lack of rapport.

Chapter Wrap-up

The 'Know, Like, and Trust' model has its place, but it's not a one-size-fits-all solution. Today's audiences demand relevance and have little patience for unnecessary buildup. To succeed, presenters need to adapt. Here's how you can move beyond the KLT model and connect more effectively:

1. **Lead with Impact:** Start with a strong hook that grabs attention and sparks thought. Skip the long introduction; dive into a compelling idea or insight that resonates with your audience's needs.

2. **Establish Credibility Fast:** Demonstrate expertise immediately through relevant stories. Utilize third-party endorsements or testimonials when possible.

3. **Challenge Comfort Zones:** Don't be afraid to push against common beliefs or present ideas that may be uncomfortable. Challenge your audience to think critically and engage deeper.

4. **Deliver Immediate Value:** Ensure your content offers practical, actionable insights your audience can use right away. Build trust by showing the usefulness of your message.

5. **Use Universal Themes:** Tap into shared human experiences—resilience, growth, change—to create an emotional connection without relying on familiarity.

6. **Customize for Relevance:** Research your audience and tailor your message to address their specific pain points or industry trends. Show you understand their context to make the message more engaging.

7. **Leverage Social Proof:** Ensure that a trusted figure introduces you or that your credentials are clearly communicated beforehand.

8. **Optimize for Attention:** Be concise and direct. Present your most important points early and reinforce them with engaging visuals, analogies, or interactive elements.

Chapter Twenty-four

Hook Your Audience From the Start With Powerful Openings

Picture yourself striding to the front of the room. The lights dim, the air buzzes with anticipation. All eyes are on you, waiting for your first words. What you do next will determine whether you seize the room's attention or lose it. In a world full of distractions, crafting a powerful opening isn't just a skill—it's essential.

For many executives, the default opening is a safe one: a polite introduction, a few remarks about the weather or the venue, and perhaps a nod to the event organizers with a 'thanks for having me.' Safe, yes. Engaging? Not so much. Your audience is filled with people who have seen and heard it all before. If you want to stand out, if you want your message to resonate long after you've left the stage, you need a better way to open.

First Impressions Are Everything

The first 30 seconds of your presentation are like the opening notes of a song—they set the tone for everything that follows. Nail this, and your audience will be tuned in for the entire performance. Fumble it, and you risk losing them before you've even begun.

Your goal should be to enchant, fascinate, captivate, and bewitch. Think of your opening as a way to hook your audience's imagination. Whether it's through humor, intrigue, or emotion, you're laying the groundwork for the rest of your presentation. Let's dive into some proven ways to open your presentation that will not only grab attention, but also set the stage for a transformative experience.

Break the Mold with a 'Hot Opening'

A 'hot opening' is a presentation technique where the presenter dives straight into the presentation with an attention-grabbing statement, story, or question, skipping preamble or housekeeping tasks. Instantly capturing the audience's attention while avoiding distractions like thank-yous or logistical notes.[38] A hot opening metaphorically lights a spark that ignites curiosity and keeps the audience engaged. You've seen it in movies and TV shows—those opening moments that make you lean in, eager for more. The magic of a hot opening lies in its unpredictability. It disrupts expectations and draws the audience's focus.

Let's explore a few types of 'hot openings' that can elevate your presentation from ordinary to extraordinary:

#1. The Provocative Question

Opening with a question can be an effective way to immediately engage your audience. But don't ask just any question. Make it one that forces the audience to think, challenges their assumptions, or sparks their curiosity.

For example: *"What if I told you that everything you know about leadership is wrong?"* This type of opening taps directly into the audience's curiosity. You've made them wonder, *"Am I wrong?"* and now they're hooked, waiting to see where you'll take them.

#2. The Bold Statement

Few things grab attention like a bold statement that defies conventional wisdom. It's audacious and begs for further explanation.

Consider this: *"In 10 years, your job won't exist."* This isn't just an attention-getter; it's a statement that demands the audience's mental engagement. Your audience is now thinking about the future and how they fit into it.

#3. The Shocking Statistic

Data can be dry—unless you know how to wield it. A shocking statistic that directly relates to your topic can ignite interest in seconds. For example: *"Did you know that 58% of executive presentations fail to make a lasting impression?"*

Now, your audience is both intrigued and, perhaps, a little worried. You've set the stage for delivering solutions.

---

[38] Interestingly, in live television this is known as a cold open.

#4. The Compelling Story

Humans are wired for storytelling. We crave narratives that help us make sense of the world. Starting your presentation with a personal or relatable story can instantly create an emotional connection with your audience.

Here's a thought: *"Five years ago, I stood on a stage just like this one, convinced I was about to make the biggest mistake of my career..."* The audience leans in. They want to know what happened next. This is the power of storytelling—creating a shared experience before you even dive into the meat of your presentation.

For a more extensive list of hot openings see Appendix A: Powerful Openers and Closers.

Note: *Craft your hot opening after developing the main body, or at least the main point of your presentation to ensure that your opening does indeed lead into your main point.*

Personalization: The Secret Sauce

One of the most impactful ways to connect with your audience is through personalization. No two audiences are the same, and neither should your presentations be. Tailor your opening to speak directly to the people in the room. This might mean referencing a recent event, quoting a conversation with someone in attendance, or acknowledging a shared experience.

For example: *"By a show of hands, who has struggled with digital transformation in your organization?"* Immediately, you've engaged your audience in an interactive way that is directly relevant to their challenges.

Humor: A Double-Edged Sword

When used correctly, humor can be one of the most effective tools in your opening arsenal. It lightens the mood, builds rapport, and makes you more relatable. However, humor is subjective, and what might land well with one audience could alienate another. If you choose to use humor, make sure it's appropriate for the audience and directly ties into your core message.

For example: *"Why did the AI cross the road? To optimize the chicken's route."* A light, industry-related humorous comment can warm up the crowd without detracting from the seriousness of your message.

The Power of Silence

Sometimes, the most impactful opening isn't words at all—it's silence. Taking a few seconds to stand silently on stage builds anticipation and focuses the room's attention on you. This unexpected pause can create a sense of curiosity. What's going to happen next? The audience is on edge, waiting for your first words.

How to Keep It Going

The beauty of a strong opening is that it gives you momentum. But remember, capturing your audience's attention is just the first step. Maintaining that attention requires a thoughtful structure, clear delivery, and continuous engagement.

Think of your presentation like a conversation. Even though you're the one speaking, involve your audience whenever possible. Ask questions, pause for reflection, and create moments where they can actively participate, even if just in their minds.

Closing the Loop

A great opening sets the stage for a memorable presentation, but don't forget about your closing. The best presenters find a way to loop back to their opening in the conclusion, creating a sense of cohesion and completion. If you started with a provocative question, answer it. If you opened with a story, bring it full circle. This technique leaves your audience feeling satisfied, like they've been taken on a journey with a meaningful destination.

Chapter Wrap-up: Your Next Step

The way you open your presentation can make all the difference between a message that resonates and one that falls flat. In today's world, where attention is a valuable commodity, exceling in the art of a captivating opening is more crucial than ever. Whether through a provocative question, a compelling story, or even a moment of silence, the right opening can captivate, engage, and ultimately transform your audience.

So, the next time you're standing in front of an audience, think carefully about your first words. They might just be the key to your presentation's—and your influence's— success.

Action Steps:

1. **Practice Different Openings:** Experiment with provocative questions, bold statements, shocking statistics, or compelling stories to determine what resonates most with your audience.

2. **Tailor Your Opening:** Research your audience and personalize your opening to reflect their interests, challenges, or recent experiences.

3. **Use Silence Strategically:** Incorporate moments of silence to build anticipation and focus attention on your message.

4. **Test Humor Carefully:** Craft a light joke or humorous anecdote relevant to your audience and test it beforehand to ensure it lands well.

5. **Record and Review:** Record your opening during practice sessions to refine your delivery and identify areas for improvement.

6. **Link Your Closing to Your Opening:** Plan your presentation to circle back to your opening, creating a cohesive and memorable experience for your audience.

7. **Seek Feedback:** After your presentation, ask trusted colleagues or audience members for feedback on your opening to continually improve.

Chapter Twenty-five

Say More With Less: How to Craft Concise, Impactful Stories

"Everything should be made as simple as possible, but no simpler." - Albert Einstein[39]

In strategic business storytelling, the power of a story lies not in its length, but in the strength and precision of its narrative. A tight, tantalizing five-minute tale that's intriguing and impactful is invariably more effective than a loose, 15-minute story that's muddled and misses the mark in mesmerizing the masses.

The key lies in being both brief and bountiful. Your story should be long enough to get its message across effectively and no longer. Each word, sentence, and element of your story should have a reason to be there. If it doesn't help move the story forward, enrich the context, add texture, evoke emotion, set the scene, or deliver the main message, it merits removal.

This idea is beautifully captured in a paraphrase of Blaise Pascal, the French mathematician and philosopher: *"I would have written a shorter letter, but I didn't have the time."*[40] It highlights the challenge and skill required to craft a concise, yet compelling story. Creating a short, impactful narrative is both an art and a discipline, requiring time and practice to perfect. A well-crafted, succinct story—clear in its message, yet rich in meaning—has far greater impact than a lengthy one that loses focus. You can also enhance your presentation by weaving in small, vivid anecdotes or micro-stories that reinforce your key points while staying aligned with your central narrative.

---

39. This quote is a paraphrased version of Einstein's original sentiment: "It can scarcely be denied that the supreme goal of all theory is to make the irreducible basic elements as simple and as few as possible without having to surrender the adequate representation of a single datum of experience." He expressed this idea during his 1933 lecture, "On the Method of Theoretical Physics," delivered at Oxford. Clearly, simplicity is often in the eye of the beholder.

40. "I had not made this longer than the rest, but that I had not the leisure to make it shorter than it is." Blaise Pascal, Les Provinciales, or, The Mystery of Jesuitisme, [Translated into English], Second Edition Corrected, 1658, Page 292, Letter 16

Action Steps:

1. **Identify Your Core Message:** Before crafting your story, clarify the main takeaway or purpose. Build your narrative around this central idea.

2. **Edit Ruthlessly:** Review your story with a critical eye. Remove any details, sentences, or elements that don't serve the main message.

3. **Practice Brevity:** Aim to tell your story in under five minutes. Record yourself and time your delivery to ensure it's concise, yet engaging.

4. **Focus on Impact:** Use vivid language and emotional hooks to make your story memorable, even if it's brief.

5. **Seek Feedback:** Share your story with a trusted colleague or mentor. Ask them to identify any parts that feel unnecessary or unclear.

6. **Rehearse for Clarity:** Practice delivering your story aloud. This helps you identify areas where the pacing or flow may need adjustment.

Chapter Twenty-six

End With Impact: Craft Closings That Leave a Lasting Impression

"If you want a happy ending, that depends, of course, on where you stop your story." - Orson Welles[41]

Knowing when and how to draw the curtain on a strategic story is an art. It's the difference between leaving your audience inspired and leaving them disenchanted. The perfect ending isn't just about wrapping things up; it's about striking the right chord at the right moment, ensuring your narrative resonates long after the final words fade.

Imagine a story that grips you, only to meander aimlessly past its climax. Or worse, one that cuts off, leaving a symphony of unresolved chords. Neither scenario does justice to the narrative or its audience. This is why the climax of your strategic business story—its moment of catharsis—must be carefully orchestrated. It's that pinnacle where conflicts dissolve, insights crystallize, and character arcs find their resolution.

A story extended beyond its natural conclusion dilutes its impact, much like overstaying a visit. It's a common pitfall, often a sign of improvisation gone awry. The key is conciseness, ensuring each word serves a purpose, each scene builds toward that final act where everything comes together in a harmonious resolution.

The art lies in balancing the narrative so that it's neither rushed nor dragged. It should conclude just as the central conflict is resolved, the lessons learned are imparted, and the call to action is made clear. It's about providing a satisfying closure, while leaving space for reflection or action, making the story not just heard, but felt and acted upon.

---

41. From the 1956 television program *The Fountain of Youth*, a proposed anthology series written, directed, and narrated by Welles. This quote neatly captures the power of choosing the right moment and method to conclude.

Such a story does more than end; it leaves a legacy. It prompts action, stirs thought, and, most importantly, sticks with the audience. Whether it's a memorable closing line that encapsulates the essence of your message, or a forward-looking perspective that paints a vision of what's to come, the conclusion should leave your audience not just satisfied, but inspired.

Crafting the end of a strategic business story, then, is about finding that sweet spot where the narrative's goals are achieved, its message delivered, and its impact felt. It's a delicate balance, requiring a keen understanding of timing, audience engagement, and the emotional journey you've taken them on.

As you pen the closing paragraphs of your business story, remember: the power of an ending lies not just in the resolution of conflict or the delivery of a key message, but in its ability to leave a lasting imprint on the hearts and minds of your audience. Choose wisely, for the right ending can transform a simple story into an unforgettable journey.

Action Steps:

1. **Identify the Climax:** Determine the most impactful moment in your story and ensure the conclusion naturally follows from this point.

2. **Keep It Concise:** Avoid adding unnecessary details after the resolution. Trim any elements that don't serve the final message.

3. **End with a Call to Action:** Provide your audience with clear next steps or a thought-provoking takeaway that encourages them to act or reflect.

4. **Craft a Memorable Closing Line:** Summarize the essence of your story in a single, impactful sentence that resonates long after the story ends. *(refer back to page 54)*

5. **Use Emotional Resonance:** Ensure your conclusion aligns with the emotional journey of your story, leaving the audience with a sense of satisfaction or inspiration.

6. **Tie Back to the Beginning:** Create a full-circle moment by connecting your ending to your story's opening, reinforcing the main theme. Or use an appropriate hot opening as a closer.

7. **Test Your Ending:** Share your story with trusted colleagues or mentors to ensure the conclusion feels impactful and cohesive.

8. **Practice Timing:** Rehearse your story to ensure the ending is neither rushed nor prolonged, maintaining a natural flow.

Chapter Twenty-seven

Ditch the Clichés: Speak Boldly to Command Attention and Credibility

Ah, the good old cliché. It's the trusty sidekick, the familiar friend you reach for when you're short on time, or worse, creativity. But let's call 'em as I see 'em: when it comes to presentations, clichés aren't just boring—they're credibility killers. You might think you're hitting the nail on the head, but in reality, you're putting your audience to sleep faster than a lullaby at naptime.

Picture this: You step on stage, clear your throat, and say, *"We need to think outside the box."* Cue the collective eye roll. Sure, it's a crowd-pleaser from a simpler time, but now? It's about as fresh as week-old bread. Your audience has heard it a thousand times before, and hearing it again is like being served the same cold dish for dinner night after night. They deserve better—and so do you.

When you use clichés, you're telling your audience that you're playing it safe. You're sticking to the well-worn path instead of blazing a new trail. They're left wondering, *"If this person can't even come up with a new way to say something, can they really help us solve complex problems?"* The answer, unfortunately, is probably no. It's not exactly confidence-inspiring.

And let's not forget the sea of vague, overused phrases: *"At the end of the day,"* *"let's take this to the next level,"* or the ever-popular *"it is what it is."* These tired expressions are not only unoriginal, but they also do nothing to enhance your message. If anything, they dilute it. They're like filling up on empty carbs before a big race—you're not fueling the conversation; you're just slowing it down.

The truth is, clichés are a crutch. They may feel like a quick fix, but they'll trip you up in the long run. Instead of relying on phrases that have lost their meaning, push yourself to dig deeper. Find new ways to express your ideas. When you do, you'll not only hold your audience's attention, but you'll also earn their respect.

Action Steps:

1. **Identify the Clichés:** Review your presentation scripts or talking points and highlight overused phrases. Replace them with specific, fresh language.

2. **Get Personal:** Use anecdotes, analogies, or vivid examples that connect directly with your audience's experiences.

3. **Add Precision:** Swap vague phrases like *"take it to the next level"* with concrete, actionable terms that clarify your point.

4. **Challenge Yourself:** Before settling on a phrase, ask, *"Is this the most original way I can say this?"* If not, keep refining.

5. **Test for Impact:** Share your updated phrasing with colleagues or friends. Does it feel engaging and authentic? Adjust based on their feedback.

6. **Practice Fresh Delivery:** Rehearse using your revised language to ensure it flows naturally and feels confident.

Chapter Twenty-eight

Excel in the Three-Act Structure: Build Stories That Drive Business Success

In previous chapters, we explored how to generate story ideas, gather raw materials, and understand your audience's unique perspective. Now, it's time to heed Robert Herrick's timeless reminder: *"Gather ye rosebuds while ye may."*[42] Crafting your stories is like weaving those rosebuds into a bouquet—an art that demands your attention while the bloom is fresh. This is your moment to connect, inspire, or persuade. So, let's gather those blooms and shape them into something truly unforgettable.

There's no universal formula for crafting a great business story. The right structure and elements depend on your message and what resonates with your audience. But here's the truth: a strategic business story doesn't need to replicate the intricate twists of a Hollywood thriller or the emotional intensity of a romance novel. Simplicity often wins. Timeless structures, like the classic three-act framework, offer the foundation for stories that stick.

While every story is unique, the underlying structure often follows familiar patterns. Ever wonder why some stories linger in your memory while others fade like a dream at dawn? It's no accident—it's structure. The three-act framework has captivated audiences for centuries, from ancient Greek dramas to modern blockbusters. Let's break it down, not with technical jargon, but as a clear and practical roadmap to elevate your next presentation, pitch, or even a casual anecdote.

---

42. The complete line is: "Gather ye rosebuds while ye may, Old Time is still a-flying." Robert Herrick, "To the Virgins, to Make Much of Time," in *Hesperides*, ed. Alfred Pollard (London: Lawrence & Bullen, 1891), 14–15.

Act 1: The Set-Up

Every great story starts by drawing you into a world—ordinary, familiar, and relatable. It introduces a central character—often called the protagonist, or hero—who will carry us through the tale. But here's a twist: the person we most identify with may not even be the main character. This 'identity character' acts as our surrogate, helping us experience the story from a deeply personal perspective.

Take *The Wizard of Oz*.[43] We meet Dorothy Gale in her quiet Kansas life—a place that's ordinary to her, but rich in context for us. The dusty plains, the farm, and the struggles of rural life set the stage. Your story's setup should do the same: immerse your audience in a relatable world while hinting at something bigger on the horizon. This world is the 'old normal.'

Act 2: The Inciting Incident and Rising Action

Then comes the spark—the moment when the familiar is shattered. For Dorothy, it's a whirlwind, quite literally, that lifts her from Kansas and drops her in Oz. Suddenly, the stakes are clear: she wants to go home. But like every compelling hero, she faces hurdles: witches, flying monkeys, and a mysterious Wizard with unclear motives.

The rising action is where your story earns its place. Conflict fuels engagement. Struggles, whether external like a fierce competitor or internal like self-doubt, are essential. And don't forget stakes—they must be high enough to make your audience care. Dorothy's ruby slippers might glitter, but they're also a constant reminder that her goal is tantalizingly close yet maddeningly out of reach.

In your own storytelling, this is where you add layers of complexity. Maybe your protagonist must pivot strategies, overcome doubt, or build alliances. Keep the momentum strong; this is the engine that pulls your audience forward.

---

43. King Vidor, Victor Fleming, George Cukor, Richard Thorpe, Norman Taurog, and Mervyn LeRoy. 1939. *The Wizard of Oz*. United States: Metro-Goldwyn-Mayer (MGM).

Act 3: The Critical Moment and Resolution

Then, it happens: the critical or, as some people call it, the aha moment. Dorothy realizes the power to return home was within her all along. Glinda, the Good Witch, reveals the truth, but not before Dorothy has endured enough to truly understand its meaning. Victory, whether earned or denied, must feel deserved.

The resolution is where transformation takes center stage. Dorothy bids her friends farewell and clicks her heels three times, returning to Kansas wiser and more appreciative of her life—the 'new normal.'. For your story, this is where you inspire your audience to see the possibilities—a call to action rooted in the lessons your hero has learned.

Here's the bottom line: whether you're pitching an idea, delivering a keynote, or telling a tale over coffee, the classic three-act structure is your secret weapon. It's not just about entertaining—it's about connecting. When you structure your stories with intention, you don't just share information; you create moments that resonate long after the final word.

The structural components of this model can be creatively described in various ways:

Classic Structure: Setup, Confrontation, Resolution.

Journey Stages: Departure, Adventure, Return.

Timeframes: Past, Present, Future.

Story Evolution: Introduction, Escalation, Climax.

Growth of a Plant: Plant, Grow, Bloom.

Project Phases: Planning, Execution, Completion.

Growth Stages in Nature: Seed, Growth, Harvest.

Character Arc: Innocence, Experience, Wisdom.

A Meal: Appetizer, Main Course, Dessert.

Conflict Phases: Tension Building, Conflict Peak, Resolution.

Emotional Arc: Curiosity, Involvement, Satisfaction.

Narrative Progression: Question, Exploration, Answer.

Scientific Method: Hypothesis, Experiment, Proof.

Life Stages: Youth, Maturity, Legacy (or Birth, Life, Death).

Problem-Solving: Identifying Issue, Addressing Issue, Resolving Issue.

Learning Process: Theory, Practice, Expertise (or Thesis, Antithesis, Synthesis).

Seasonal Metaphor: Spring (Beginning), Summer (Middle), Autumn and Winter (End).

Each metaphor encapsulates the essence of the three-act structure in a unique context, offering a fresh perspective on the classic beginning, middle, and end format.

The Hero's Journey

A more modern and expanded storytelling framework is the Hero's Journey, famously described by Joseph Campbell in *The Hero with a Thousand Faces*.[44] This universal narrative structure underpins countless myths, legends, and stories across cultures, offering a timeless blueprint for transformation and growth.

The Hero's Journey follows a central character—referred to as the hero—on an extraordinary adventure that begins in their ordinary world—the 'old normal.' Their journey starts with **The Call to Adventure**, a challenge or quest that pulls them away from the familiar. Though often hesitant, the hero eventually steps forward, aided by a mentor or guide who provides tools, wisdom, or encouragement. Crossing the threshold, they enter the unknown—a realm brimming with trials, allies, enemies, and opportunities for growth.

---

44. Joseph Campbell, The Hero with a Thousand Faces (New York: Pantheon Books, 1949)

At the core of the journey lies the **Abyss or Ordeal**, a pivotal moment where the hero confronts their greatest fear or challenge. This experience, akin to a symbolic death and rebirth, results in profound transformation, granting the hero newfound insight, strength, or power.

The final stage is **The Return**, where the hero brings their hard-earned wisdom or treasure back to their ordinary world. This return often involves sharing their discoveries with others, restoring balance, or reshaping their community—the 'new normal.' The Hero's Journey, at its heart, is a tale of personal and universal transformation, revealing the boundless potential within us all.

Speaker and TED presenter Nancy Duarte emphasizes that in every presentation, the presenter plays the role of mentor, while the audience steps into the hero's shoes.[45] When applying the Hero's Journey to your story, it can unfold like this: **The Hero—your customer—embarks on an adventure.** They face a critical problem and need a guide to help them navigate the challenge. That's you. Along the way, they experience a critical moment, gaining new insight or knowledge. Armed with this discovery, they overcome their obstacle and achieve victory. Finally, they return home transformed, stepping into their 'new normal' with newfound confidence and success.

This storytelling approach transforms presentations into engaging, transformative experiences, ensuring your audience doesn't just hear the message, but feels it, lives it, and remembers it.

So, what's your story? Will it captivate, or will it fade like a whisper in the wind? You've got the blueprint. Now go build something unforgettable.

Note: *For a story creation outline see "Appendix B: Outline for Crafting a Story:" on page 249.*

---

45. Nancy Duarte, *Resonate: Present Visual Stories that Transform Audiences* (Hoboken, NJ: Wiley, 2010)

Part Seven
Dynamic Delivery

In an episode of the Banacek TV series,[46] a memorable exchange takes place in Felix Mulholland's cozy rare book store. Banacek, a sharp-witted freelance insurance investigator, stands amid the shelves of antique volumes, casting a quizzical look at Mulholland—a rare book dealer and trusted confidant—comfortably seated in his wingback easy chair. With pride, Mulholland declares, *"I'm learning karate."* Banacek responds with a skeptical retort: *"Sitting down?"* Felix, catching the subtle jab, counters with mock indignation, *"Do I detect a note of cynicism in your voice?"* Banacek delivers the final words with his signature wit: *"I took combat judo in the Marine Corps, but as I remember, they didn't issue us any easy chairs."*

This exchange underscores a universal truth: developing expertise isn't a passive process. Whether you're crafting a story, delivering a presentation, or learning karate, you can't sit back and expect progress to come to you. You have to actively engage, take risks, and embrace the discomfort that comes with improvement.

> *"You don't become a better storyteller by reading this book. You get there by completing the action steps, practicing, and telling stories."*

Reading can inspire and inform, but real growth happens in the doing. It's in the moments when you stumble over your words, discover the perfect pause, or adapt to your audience's reactions. Like any skill, storytelling requires practice—repeated, intentional, and sometimes messy practice.

The lessons in this book will guide you, but transformation happens when you take them off the page and put them into action—into your voice, your gestures, and your connection with the audience. Only then can you truly grow as a storyteller and communicator.

---

46. "Project Phoenix," Banacek, season 1, episode 3, directed by Paul Krasny, aired September 27, 1972, on NBC.

Influence Amplified

In this section, we build on the foundations of story crafting and presentation structure explored in earlier sections. By combining those principles with vivid storytelling, intentional presence, and technical expertise, these chapters delve into the art of delivering impactful stories. From refining the nuances of vocal dynamics to using eye contact that engages and energizes, you'll learn how to adapt to any environment—whether commanding a grand stage, leading a virtual meeting, or addressing a boardroom. Packed with actionable insights, this section empowers you to own the room, inspire your audience, and amplify your message.

Get ready to step into your full potential as a communicator—someone who doesn't just speak, but leaves an indelible impact.

Chapter Twenty-nine

From Vocalizing to Captivating: Secrets from a Galaxy Far, Far Away

"The ability to speak does not make you intelligent." —Qui-Gon Jinn[47]

This iconic line from *Star Wars: Episode I – The Phantom Menace* is more than just cinematic wisdom. It holds a universal truth that stretches far beyond the galaxy far, far away. It begs the question: does the ability to vocalize inherently make you an effective presenter or storyteller? Not at all. Talking is easy; captivating is an art.

Consider this: just because words come out of your mouth doesn't mean they make sense, resonate, or engage. As Merriam-Webster succinctly puts it, *"Having a faculty for speech is not the same as having a facility for speech."*[48] The essence of impactful communication lies far deeper.

Speaking is a physical act—a vocalization of thought. But inspiring and engaging others? That's a crafted experience, an intentional combination of skill, passion, and authenticity. Whether addressing one person or an audience of thousands, your words, your tone, and the energy behind your message can create something much greater than just speech.

---

[47]. A stunning rebuke uttered by Qui-Gon Jinn (played by Liam Nesson) at Jar Jar Binks (voiced by Ahmed Best) from the 1999 sci-fi film Star Wars: Episode I – The Phantom Menace, written and directed by George Lucas. Possibly paraphrasing an old Yiddish saying, "Just because you can talk, it doesn't mean you're making sense."

[48]. Paraphrasing: "Having a faculty for speech means you can communicate by enunciating words and stringing them together. But having a facility for speech suggests that you can speak with a particular eloquence, the kind that might hold an audience's attention. Merriam-Webster, "Facility vs. Faculty: What's the Difference and When to Use Each?" *Merriam-Webster.com*, https://www.merriam-webster.com/grammar/facility-vs-faculty-difference-usage.

The Art of Storytelling

Storytelling is not a feat to be 'winged.' It's an art form—a deliberate and practiced craft. Effective storytelling paints vivid pictures with words, forging emotional connections and transforming abstract ideas into tangible experiences for your audience. Every word, every pause, every inflection is a stroke in this intricate work of art. The goal is not just to inform, but to ignite, to create a story that lives and breathes in the imagination of your listeners.

Think of storytelling as a symphony. Each element—the rhythm of language, the power of silence, the rise and fall of your tone—works together to create an emotional journey. Knowing when to amplify your voice for emphasis and when to let it drop to a whisper can draw your audience in, holding their attention as if by magic.

Illusion of Spontaneity

A well-delivered story feels spontaneous, not scripted—but that spontaneity is an illusion. Achieving a fresh, natural delivery requires deliberate and intentional practice. To create this effect, don't perform or merely recount the story. Instead, re-live it. Invite the audience to experience the story with you, as if it's unfolding in real-time, rather than as a memory from the past.

Beyond Words: The Unseen Threads

Great communication is not just about what you say; it's about how you say it. Your body language, eye contact, and the conviction in your tone are the unseen threads that bind your message to your audience's hearts and minds. The way you carry yourself on stage or in a meeting can either amplify your words or render them meaningless.

Beyond eye contact and posture, non-verbal cues like micro-expressions and tone shifts reveal your authenticity. A slight raise of an eyebrow can signal curiosity, while an intentional pause adds emphasis. To refine these skills, record yourself and review how your body language reinforces or contradicts your words. When aligned, these subtle signals amplify your Executive Presence.

Think of these elements as the stage on which your words perform. A well-timed gesture, a confident posture, or a moment of intentional stillness can amplify your message far more than the words alone. These nonverbal cues tell your audience, *"This matters."*

Intelligence in Action

As you reflect on that line from Star Wars or the Merriam-Webster quote, let them remind you that the ability to vocalize is merely the starting point. True intelligence and expertise in communication lie in using that ability to touch, inspire, and transform. Speaking with intention is about more than words; it's about creating moments of connection and resonance.

Embrace this journey with the enthusiasm of a learner and the heart of an artist. Your voice—used with skill and purpose—can be a powerful force for change, both in your world and the worlds of those you touch.

Action Steps:

1. **Craft Your Narrative:** Practice crafting stories with clear beginnings, middles, and ends. Identify the emotions you want to evoke and the key takeaways for your audience.

2. **Strengthen Your Nonverbal Communication:** Pay attention to your body language, eye contact, and tone of voice. Record yourself and evaluate these elements alongside your words.

3. **Experiment with Pacing:** Practice varying your pace and tone. Use the power of your voice to emphasize key points, and pauses to let ideas sink in.

4. **Seek Feedback:** Deliver your story to a trusted peer or mentor. Ask for specific feedback on your delivery, narrative flow, and engagement.

5. **Reflect and Refine:** After each speaking opportunity, reflect on what worked and what didn't. Incorporate these insights into your next presentation.

Chapter Thirty

Command the Room: Unlocking Executive Presence with the Six Ss

When Priya stepped onto the stage for the first time at her company's annual leadership summit, her heart raced. She had spent weeks perfecting her content, ensuring every slide was polished and every point sharp. But as she looked out at the audience—a sea of expectant faces—she realized something critical: it wasn't just about what she would say. It was about how she showed up.

Executive Presence isn't a mystical trait bestowed upon a select few. It's a skill—a combination of behaviors and attitudes that command attention, build trust, and inspire action. And while many might think of it as intangible, it can be unlocked with a simple framework: the Six Ss. These six steps—Stride, Stand, Settle, Sweep, Smile, and Speak—serve as your blueprint for captivating an audience from the very first moment. Let's explore how each one transforms a presenter into a leader.

1. Stride

Imagine this: You're being introduced, and all eyes turn toward you. Your first few steps onto the stage send a message before you utter a single word. Will it be a message of confidence or hesitation? The way you enter sets the tone for everything that follows.[49]

Stride isn't just about walking; it's about owning the space. Priya recalled a time when she shuffled nervously into a meeting, instantly diminishing her credibility. This time, she squared her shoulders, lifted her chin, and took deliberate steps to center stage. Her entrance said, *"I'm ready. I'm here to lead."*

---

[49]. From the moment members of your audience hear about you, you are being judged. If they first hear about you during your introduction, that's also when the judgment begins. That judgment continues as you take the stage. Therefore, it is necessary to step onto the stage and command the room with confidence. That's what the six Ss do for you. They help you exude confidence.

Influence Amplified

"Your energy introduces you before you even speak." **African proverb**

Even in virtual presentations, the principle applies. As soon as the camera turns on, your posture, facial expression, and energy must convey that you're present and ready to engage. Stride—physically or virtually—signals your readiness and leadership.

2. Stand

Once you've taken your position on stage, at the front of the room, or in front of the camera, it's time to anchor yourself. Your stance communicates just as much as your words. Adopt the **Neutral Stance**:[50] Stand tall with your shoulders back and feet shoulder-width apart, pointing straight ahead or slightly outward for comfort. Keep your arms relaxed at your sides and distribute your weight evenly between both feet, and slightly forward. Maintain a slight bend in your knees—never locked—while keeping your hips and shoulders aligned. While this posture may feel unfamiliar at first, it promotes balance, stability, and readiness for movement in any direction. Most importantly, it conveys presence and poise.

Social psychologist Amy Cuddy's research on power posing[51] underscores the transformative power of posture. Priya practiced the "Power Pose" backstage, grounding herself in confidence and composure. When she stepped onto the stage and shifted into the Neutral Stance, her commanding presence and self-assured delivery demonstrated just how impactful these techniques can be in action.

When you stand with intention, you project authority and credibility, creating a powerful foundation for connection and influence.

---

50. The term "neutral stance" is commonly used across various fields, including speaking, martial arts, and physical therapy. It is referred to as *Heiko Dachi* in Japanese..
51. Dana R. Carney, Amy J.C. Cuddy, and Andy J. Yap. "Power Posing: Brief Nonverbal Displays Affect Neuroendocrine Levels and Risk Tolerance." *Psychological Science* 21, no. 10 (2010): 1363–68. Amy Cuddy, "Your Body Language Shapes Who You Are," *TED*, filmed June 2012, published October 2012, https://www.ted.com/talks/amy_cuddy_your_body_language_shapes_who_you_are.

3. Settle

The instinct to launch into your presentation immediately can be tempting. But the third S—**Settle**—teaches us the power of the pause. After your stride and stand, take a moment. Stand still. Let the audience adjust to your presence. It may feel like an eternity, but it will only take a few seconds.

Priya learned that silence isn't awkward; it's powerful. Those few seconds allowed her to gather her thoughts and let the audience focus entirely on her. The room's energy shifted, creating a space of anticipation. When you're comfortable with stillness, you exude authority, and your audience leans in, ready to hear what you have to say.

The Power of Constructive Discomfort

People I coach often admit, *"I'm not really comfortable standing in silence."* My response? Discomfort is a natural part of growth. In fact, many elements of developing Executive Presence—like commanding silence, refining delivery, or honing body language—may feel awkward at first.

Warren Buffett, the *Oracle of Omaha*, offers timeless advice that ties directly into this idea: *"The one easy way to become worth 50 percent more than you are now, at least, is to hone your communication skills–both written and verbal."*[52] Buffett's wisdom underscores a vital truth: growth requires stepping outside your comfort zone, especially when it comes to communication.

If the thought of speaking in front of an audience fills you with dread, consider this: what if that uneasiness wasn't something to fear, but a form of *constructive discomfort*?[53] Reframing it this way can be transformative. It's in those challenging moments—when you step beyond the familiar—that meaningful progress truly begins.

---

52. Warren Buffett shared this advice during a conversation with Michael Hood, co-founder of the Toronto-based start-up Voiceflow as they were riding together in a car. Hood posted a video of their interaction on LinkedIn in December 2018. The story was picked-up by Inc. Schwantes, Marcel. "Warren Buffett Says Improving This 1 Skill We Use Every Day Will Increase Your Worth by 50 Percent." *Inc.*, December 4, 2018. https://www.inc.com/marcel-schwantes/warren-buffett-says-improving-this-1-skill-we-use-every-day-will-increase-your-worth-by-50-percent.html.
53. A term prevalent in various fields, including psychology and education.

Influence Amplified

As Peter McWilliams wisely said, *"Comfort zones are most often expanded through discomfort."*[54] To grow, it's essential to *"learn to get comfortable with being uncomfortable."*[55] Discomfort isn't a roadblock; it's a signal that you're pushing boundaries and moving forward. Viewed as a catalyst for growth rather than an obstacle, it becomes a powerful ally in your journey to amplify your presence, refine your skills, and unlock your full potential.

"Elevate your confidence to match your competence."

4. Sweep

Connection is the foundation of communication, and Sweep brings it to life. It's about turning your entire body and sweeping the audience—making deliberate, meaningful eye-to-eye and heart-to-heart contact with each person, to create inclusivity. Priya likened it to a dance, where every movement acknowledged someone in the room. Her sweep wasn't just a gesture; it was a bridge connecting her with everyone in the room, ensuring no one felt left out. Each audience member became her partner, and her deliberate focus made them feel part of her story, acknowledged and valued. *(see "The Art of Heart-to-Heart Connection: Lessons from Robert Fripp" on page 189)*

Even in virtual settings, this principle holds. Priya learned to look directly into the camera lens, imagining it as the eyes of every participant. This simple act transformed her delivery, creating a sense of intimacy that made even remote attendees feel seen and valued.

5. Smile

A genuine smile can disarm even the most skeptical audience. It's a universal signal of warmth and approachability. Priya practiced smiling before her presentation, not out of obligation, but as an expression of her enthusiasm.

A smile isn't just about your lips; it's about your energy. It communicates, *"I'm glad to be here with you."* For Priya, her smile melted the initial tension in the room, inviting her audience to join her on the journey she was about to lead.

---

54. John Roger McWilliams. Peter McWilliams. Life 101: Everything We Wish We Had Learned about Life in School--but Didn't. United States: Prelude Press, 1991.
55. The phrase "Get comfortable being uncomfortable" is widely used across various fields, from sports to business and personal development though its exact origin is unclear.

6. Speak

Finally, the moment arrives. The way you open your presentation determines whether you'll captivate your audience or lose them. Priya had learned to skip the mundane pleasantries. Instead, she dove directly into the core of her presentation with a compelling story, the strongest of hot openings—a moment of failure that taught her a critical lesson about leadership.

A 'Hot Opening'— (page 143) whether it's a provocative question, surprising statistic, or vivid anecdote—grabs attention immediately. It's the hook that makes people lean in, eager to hear more. Priya's story not only resonated, but also set the stage for her key points. By speaking with purpose and passion, she made her message unforgettable.

The Six Ss in Action

When Priya finished her presentation, the applause wasn't just polite; it was enthusiastic. People approached her afterward, not just to compliment her content, but to praise how she delivered it. She had perfected the Six Ss, turning a presentation into an experience.

The Six Ss—Stride, Stand, Settle, Sweep, Smile, and Speak—aren't just techniques; they're tools for unlocking Executive Presence. They remind us that how we show up matters as much as what we say. By integrating these steps into your presentations, you're not just sharing information; you're inspiring your audience, building trust, and leading with impact.

So, the next time you step onto a stage or log into a virtual meeting, remember Priya's journey. Take that confident stride. Stand tall. Settle into the moment. Sweep the room to make connections. Smile with authenticity. And speak with purpose. These six simple actions can transform how others see you—and how you see yourself. That's the power of Executive Presence.

Action Steps:

1. **Practice Your Stride:** Work on entering rooms and stages with confidence, even in virtual settings. Start with deliberate, grounded movements that convey readiness.

2. **Perfect Your Posture:** Use the Neutral Stance to prepare for presentations, and focus on standing with intention to project authority.

3. **Polish the Pause:** Before speaking, practice pausing to gather your thoughts and let your presence settle over the room.

4. **Engage Through Eye Contact:** Whether in person or virtually, make deliberate eye contact to connect with your audience.

5. **Share Your Smile:** Reflect genuine enthusiasm and approachability with a warm, authentic smile.

6. **Refine Your Openings:** Experiment with 'Hot Openings' to grab attention right away and set the stage for a compelling message.

Note: *Your official presentation might begin with your introduction and end when you leave the stage, but your whole presentation actually starts the moment you agree to speak or set up the meeting where you'll be speaking. And it doesn't stop when you finish speaking; it continues afterwards as you follow-up with your audience.*

Chapter Thirty-one

Refining The 'Unspoken' Elements of Delivery

Have you ever watched a presenter and felt something was off, even when their words were flawless? Their arms hang stiffly, their movements feel mechanical, and their gestures don't quite match the story. You don't just hear the disconnect—you feel it. Now picture the opposite: a presenter whose gestures amplify their message, drawing you into their story. Which one are you more likely to trust and remember?

The Power of Hands

Gestures are more than just hand movements—they're visual punctuation marks that underscore your message. Research[56] shows people who use their hands while speaking are perceived as warm, energetic, and trustworthy—all great components of Executive Presence. Your gestures can clarify your ideas, reinforce your energy, and engage your audience in ways words alone cannot. But here's the catch: they need to be intentional.

> *"A picture is worth a thousand words, and so is an appropriate gesture."*

The 'gesture zone'[57] is your ideal space for impactful gestures. Imagine it as a heart shape, with the bottom tip flipped upward and a notch at the top that aligns with the size of your face. Starting from a Neutral Stance *(page 170)* with your arms at your sides, the zone spans from your fingertips up to your belly button. It extends outward to the tips of your outstretched arms and upward to the top of your head, while deliberately excluding the

---

56. Carolyn Gregoire, "The Fascinating Science Behind 'Talking' With Your Hands," Huffington Post, February 4, 2016, https://www.huffpost.com/entry/talking-with-hands-gestures_n_56afcfaae4b0b8d7c230414e.
57. Carmine Gallo refers to the "power sphere," Talk Like TED: The 9 Public-Speaking Secrets of the World's Top Minds (New York: St. Martin's Press, 2014), 98. Several authors and communication experts have coined terms for the area within which presenters can gesture to maximize impact and audience engagement. They include: Vanessa Van Edwards - "The Truth Plane" Allan and Barbara Pease - "Gesture Box" Deborah Gruenfeld - "Zone of Authority" and Julius Fast - "The Key Zone"

space directly in front of your face. The idea is to 'frame your face' rather than obscure it.[58] If you're presenting on camera, the outside edges of your gesture zone are confined to the limits of the camera frame.

Within this zone, your gestures are viewed by the audience as natural and authoritative. When you gesture here, you're not just amplifying your words—you're anchoring your presence.

To make full use of this zone, if you have the choice, stand while presenting.

Avoiding the Gesture Traps

Not all hand movements are created equal. Some can sabotage your Executive Presence faster than you realize.

- **Hands in Pockets**: Comfortable? Sure. But it signals you're hiding something, undermining trust.[59]
- **The 'Fig Leaf'**: Resting your hands together low in front of you is a common default stance, but it can unintentionally signal nervousness or hesitation.
- **Overused Gestures**: Repeatedly clasping your hands in prayer or using the 'steeple' can seem contrived, even manipulative.
- **Make a Point, But Don't Point**: It's not polite to point your finger. If you must indicate someone or something, always point with two fingers or your entire hand — a gesture known as "The Disney Point."[60]

The solution isn't to choreograph your every move. Instead, re-live the emotions of your story. When you re-experience the excitement, urgency, or reflection, your gestures will arise naturally, making them feel authentic.

Note: *For a list of positive and negative gestures, see "Appendix C: Hand Gestures for Executive Presence and Presentation Skills" on page 253.*

---

58. Positioning your body and gestures so your face remains visible is known as "staying open" in filmmaking, and "cheating out" in theater.
59. Joe Navarro. "Body Language of the Hands." Psychology Today, January 20, 2010, https://www.psychologytoday.com/ca/blog/spycatcher/201001/body-language-the-hands.
60. In many cultures, pointing with one finger is considered rude. Since Disney World hosts guests from all over the world, the resort teaches its employees to be sensitive to these cultural differences and never point with one finger. An internal practice that gradually became known to the public over time.

Movement That Commands Attention[61]

Movement on stage isn't just about filling space—it's about owning it. Strategic movement signals confidence, helps structure your message, and keeps your audience engaged.

> *"Suiting the action to the word, the word to the action."*[62]

Here's a simple rule: move with purpose. Shift when transitioning to a new idea, delivering a story, or emphasizing a key point. And when it's time to land your punchlines and make your point? Plant your feet. A strong Neutral Stance (see page 170) reinforces the gravity of your words, allowing your audience to focus entirely on your message.

> *"Unmotivated movements are distracting. Motivated movement is dramatic and captivating. If you move, move with conviction."*

A Stage as a Timeline

If your presentation involves a sequence of events, use the stage to represent time. Picture a timeline stretching across the stage: when addressing cultures that read left to right, moving to your audience's left signifies the past, while moving to their right indicates the future. This spatial storytelling adds depth and clarity, giving your audience a mental map to follow.

Expressions that Speak Volumes

Your face tells a story long before you open your mouth. The smallest mismatch between your words and your expression can create confusion. If you say, *"I'm thrilled to be here,"* but your face is neutral or tense, the audience will sense the disconnect. Practice aligning your expressions with your message.[63]

The secret? Develop your "Mona Lisa face"[64]—neutral, approachable, and thoughtful. It gives you time to think without revealing every emotion while maintaining a connection with your audience.

---

61. You may see and hear the terms staging and blocking. Staging is the process of moving around a stage. Blacking is the process of deciding where you'll be at a given point in your presentation.
62. William Shakespeare, Hamlet, Act 3 Scene 2.
63. Qu, Fangbing, et al. "'You Should Have Seen the Look on Your Face…': Self-awareness of Facial Expressions." Frontiers in Psychology, May 30, 2017, https://www.frontiersin.org/articles/10.3389/fpsyg.2017.00832/full.
64. Nwaz, Sabina. "Want to Be a Successful Leader? Try Changing Your Facial Expressions." Inc.com, March 14, 2017, https://www.inc.com/sabina-nawaz/how-your-facial-expressions-may-be-undermining-your-leadership.html.

Microphone Technique

If you're using a handheld microphone, using it effectively can make or break your presentation. Hold the microphone about 6–8 inches from your mouth, and at a slight angle to avoid plosive sounds, like harsh "P" or "B" pops. Maintain a consistent distance to ensure your voice stays clear and audible, adjusting only slightly for dramatic emphasis or projection. Avoid gripping the microphone too tightly or waving it around, as this creates distracting noise. Most importantly, conduct a sound check beforehand to align your speaking volume with the microphone's sensitivity—poor technique can muffle your words or overpower the audience, undermining even the best-prepared content.

Action Steps:

1. **Gesture Zone Practice:** Stand in front of a mirror and practice gestures within the zone. Speak aloud, matching your movements to your words.

2. **Gesture Audit**: Record yourself giving a presentation. Watch for distracting gestures like hands in pockets, fig leaf, or overused hand movements.

3. **Own the Space**: Practice walking across a room as you transition between points. Stop and plant yourself firmly when delivering key messages.

4. **Facial Awareness**: Use a video recording to observe your expressions. Practice aligning them with the tone and emotion of your presentation.

5. **Timeline Staging**: Map your presentation on an imaginary stage timeline, assigning sections of the stage to different parts of your story.

Chapter Wrap-up:

Every movement, gesture, and expression tells a story—whether you intend it to or not. By becoming intentional about how you use your body, you don't just enhance your Executive Presence—you transform it. So, as you prepare for your next presentation, ask yourself: are your gestures reinforcing your message or competing with it?

Chapter Thirty-two

Beyond Words: Use Vocal Shading to Captivate and Connect

"Words, words, words." – Shakespeare[65]

A story's true soul—and power to influence—lies in its ability to forge a deep connection—emotionally and intellectually—with its audience. A great story leaves an unforgettable mark, inspiring thought, sparking action, and moving hearts and minds. Shakespeare,[66] a maestro of language, demonstrated the timeless power of well-crafted words. Yet even he understood that the impact of a story isn't just in its content; it's in how that content resonates with the audience.

So, what makes a story unforgettable? It's not just the words you choose, but how you deliver them. The saying, *"It's not what you say, but how you say it,"*[67] encapsulates the secret. Your voice is more than a tool; it's an intricate instrument, blending the richness of wind and string instruments to add depth and complexity to your narrative.

In the art of speaking, **vocal shading**[68] is your ace. It cuts through distractions, captivates attention, and ensures your message lingers long after your presentation ends. Let's explore how to enhance your storytelling with vocal shading:

1. Pace

Control the rhythm of your speech. A measured pace invites your audience to fully absorb your message; while varying it can evoke urgency or introspection. Slow down to emphasize key points or speed up to build excitement. Your pace sets the mood.

---

65. Hamlet: Act 2, Scene 2. Hamlet's reply to Polonius.
66. Born April 23, 1564. Died April 23, 1616.
67. I thought my mother coined this pearl of wisdom, but it's actually from "Talks on Trade Topics." An article by Hugh Kalyptus. The Australian Saddler and Harness Maker, June 1, 1912. Page 262.
68. A descriptive term borrowed from the field of vocal music to describe various techniques and nuances in singing. E.g., Dwight's Journal of Music - Volumes 31-32, 1873. Page 275.

2. Pitch

The tonal variation of your voice brings your story to life. Use pitch to express a spectrum of emotions and emphasize critical points. A well-placed rise or drop in tone adds dynamism to your delivery and keeps your audience engaged.

3. Projection

Volume matters. Adjust your voice to underscore significant points, whether you're conveying excitement with a louder projection or creating intimacy by lowering your voice. Projection helps carry your emotions across the room.

4. Rhythm

Diverse speech patterns energize your presentation. Rhythm creates movement and flow, drawing listeners into your story. Think of it as the heartbeat of your delivery—steady, deliberate, and alive.

5. Tone

The emotional timbre of your voice establishes trust and connection. A warm, sincere tone can build rapport, while a sharp or cold tone can distance your audience. Your tone reflects your authenticity and intent.

6. Timbre

Your voice's unique qualities—its texture and resonance—make it memorable. Whether it's smooth like Barack Obama's or commanding like James Earl Jones', harness your timbre to leave a lasting impression.

7. Emotional Intensity

Show your passion. Enthusiasm and conviction are contagious. When your emotional intensity matches your message, you captivate your audience and make your narrative compelling and persuasive.

8. Pronunciation and Articulation

Clear enunciation enhances your credibility and ensures your audience understands and remembers your message. Don't let poor pronunciation or mumbling undermine your words' impact.

9. The Power of the Pause

Strategic pauses are like the white space in design—they provide your audience with the space to reflect and absorb your message. As Robert Fripp[69] famously said, *"Music is not in the notes, but in the spaces between them."* A well-timed pause can be as impactful as your words, and more so than filling the silence with "um," "uh," or "like."

While pausing for two or three seconds may feel like an eternity to you, your audience won't consciously notice. Use pauses thoughtfully: pause to encourage reflection, pause to gauge understanding, and pause to emphasize key points. These moments of silence allow your audience to absorb your message without feeling awkward.

Pause just before delivering an important statement to build anticipation, and immediately after to give your audience time to reflect. Shorter pauses—less than two seconds—can create rhythm, while longer pauses of four to five seconds are best reserved for moments of dramatic impact. Adjust the length of your pauses based on the tone of your presentation and the level of audience engagement.

There are four key moments when silence is essential: when your audience is laughing, crying, thinking, or applauding. Stand silently in the neutral stance and let them fully experience the moment before moving on. These pauses honor their reactions, making your message more resonant.

Remember, your pauses are also the audience's opportunity to contribute to the conversation—even if only in their own minds. By giving them time to recognize and organize their thoughts, you invite deeper engagement. Pausing isn't just about timing; it's about giving your audience their turn to process, connect, and participate.

---

69. Musician and King Crimson founder.

Becoming Accomplished in the Art of Vocal Shading

To excel as a storyteller, you must develop your abilities in the art of vocal shading. Use your voice—and the silence between words—to paint a vivid, compelling narrative. The power of your voice lies not only in what is spoken, but also in what is left unsaid.

Action Steps:

1. **Practice Vocal Dynamics:** Record yourself reading a short passage. Experiment with pace, pitch, and tone to discover how different dynamics affect your delivery.

2. **Use Silence Intentionally:** Add pauses to your presentation. Practice delivering a key point, then pausing for a moment to let it resonate.

3. **Enhance Your Timbre:** Identify what makes your voice unique and practice emphasizing its qualities. A voice coach or mentor can help refine your timbre.

4. **Refine Pronunciation:** Choose a complex passage and focus on enunciating every word clearly. Repeat until your delivery feels natural and precise.

5. **Express Emotion:** Identify moments in your presentation where emotional intensity can amplify your message. Practice delivering these points with conviction.

Chapter Thirty-three

The Secret to Making Meaningful Eye Contact to Enhance Your Impact

As you stand before your audience, delivering your presentation, one simple yet powerful action can captivate them and elevate your message: meaningful eye contact. This small, but impactful gesture can significantly enhance your presence and effectiveness as a presenter.

Creating Engagement

Eye contact is essential for engagement. It makes your audience feel involved and valued, boosting their attention and interest. By looking into their eyes, you project confidence, sincerity, and credibility, making your message more believable.

Consistent eye contact conveys comfort and control, improving audience perception. It enhances communication by adding clarity and emotion, allowing your audience to connect with your expressions as you share your stories. Eye contact keeps your presentation lively, interactive, and focused. It even triggers trust-building neurotransmitters like oxytocin and dopamine, deepening the connection.

Trust and Personal Connection

Trust is vital for Executive Presence, and it begins with eye contact. Eye contact fosters a personal connection and rapport. People trust and follow presenters who appear self-assured and genuine. When your audience feels seen and appreciated, the bond between you strengthens.

Improving Delivery

Eye contact improves delivery. It lets you gauge audience reactions and adjust on the fly, ensuring your message resonates. Observing your audience—known as 'reading the room' *(page 66)*—enables real-time adjustments, enhancing your presentation's effectiveness and making your delivery more polished.

Dive Deeper into Effective Eye Contact

Maintaining eye contact during a presentation can feel unnatural or uncomfortable, making it tempting to look at nothing or no one. You might have heard two outdated myths for overcoming speaking fear: imagining your audience in their underwear—which is distracting—or looking at a clock—which creates a disconnect.

Patterns for Effective Eye Contact

1. **Sequential**: Make eye contact with one person for a moment, then shift your gaze to the next. This involves everyone. For example, in a U-shaped seating arrangement of 20 people, make eye contact with each person briefly to connect, then move on. Once you've made eye contact with each person, repeat.
2. **Triangle**: Divide the audience into three sections—left, center, and right. Alternate your gaze between sections to ensure everyone feels included.
3. **Zig-Zag**: Move your eye contact across the audience in a zigzag pattern to spread your attention evenly. Once you've made eye contact with each person, repeat.
4. **Zones**: For large audiences, mentally divide the room into zones and make eye contact with one person from each zone. Once you've made eye contact with each zone, repeat.

Eye contact involves holding and moving. Look into someone's eyes to connect, then shift. Maintain eye contact for the length of a thought or a sentence, about three to five seconds. This creates a meaningful connection without discomfort.

Use sentences as natural points to switch focus. Make eye contact intentional and varied; avoid always moving from right to left or front to back. Mix it up to keep it spontaneous.

Never let your eyes glaze over. Make eye contact with someone, then shift to another person. Don't stare at one person for too long. Avoid focusing on objects or empty spaces. In intimate settings, hold eye contact with one person for up to a paragraph, then shift. For close audience members, look at one eye at a time and switch casually.

As the saying goes, *"Too much of a good thing can be bad."*[70] Prolonged eye contact, for example, can increase resistance to persuasion, especially when listeners initially disagree with your viewpoint. In adversarial situations, it may come across as dominance or intimidation, fostering skepticism and reducing receptiveness to your message.[71]

Cultural Differences

So far, we've discussed eye contact techniques primarily in Western and European contexts. Eye contact norms vary significantly across cultures:

- **Western Cultures:** In the U.S. and much of Europe, direct eye contact signifies confidence, honesty, and engagement. Presenters are encouraged to maintain eye contact to establish connection and sincerity.

- **East Asian Cultures:** In Japan, China, and Korea, prolonged eye contact can be seen as rude or confrontational. Presenters may use indirect eye contact or look slightly away to show respect.

- **Middle Eastern Cultures:** Eye contact norms vary; maintaining eye contact is often seen as respectful and sincere, especially in same-gender interactions. Gender dynamics may affect eye contact.

- **African Cultures:** Eye contact appropriateness depends on age and status. Direct eye contact might be disrespectful when addressing elders or superiors, but is acceptable among peers.

- **Latin American Cultures:** Eye contact shows interest and respect, similar to Western norms, but there is a cultural appreciation for warmth and personal connection.

- **South Asian Cultures:** In India, urban and professional settings encourage direct eye contact, while traditional or rural settings may view avoiding eye contact as respectful.

Understanding cultural nuances helps you adjust eye contact techniques to connect with your audience appropriately.

---

70. Paraphrasing "Why then, can one desire too much of a good thing?" Shakespeare, William. As You Like it: A Comedy. United Kingdom: S. Gosnell, 1810. Act IV, Scene III, page 53
71. Frances S. Chen, Julia A. Minson, Maren Schöne, and Markus Heinrichs. "In the Eye of the Beholder: Eye Contact Increases Resistance to Persuasion." *Psychological Science* 24, no. 11 (2013): 2254–61. https://chenlab-psych.sites.olt.ubc.ca/files/2013/10/Psychological-Science-2013-Chen-2254-61.pdf.

Advanced Tips for Making Eye Contact

1. **Ease into Eye Contact:** Start with someone who's looking down to make initial contact. Then engage others as well.

2. **Glance Down if Needed:** It's okay to glance at notes and then re-establish eye contact. This keeps you on track without losing engagement.

3. **Connect Individually:** Treat your audience as individuals. Think of it as a conversation with each person, not a group.

4. **Sweeping Gaze:** Periodically sweep your gaze across the audience to include everyone and maintain a steady rhythm.

5. **Lead with Your Eyes:** Avoid snapping your head from person to person. Let your eyes guide your movements naturally.

6. **Story Reenactment:** When reenacting a story, make eye contact with the imagined characters rather than the audience.

7. **Camera Tips for Video Calls:** Position your camera at eye level, then look directly at the lens to simulate eye contact.

8. **Practice and Prepare:** Rehearsing your presentation minimizes the need to look away, keeping you connected.

Exercises to Practice Eye Contact

Eye contact is a powerful tool, but becoming accomplished at it takes practice. Here are some exercises to build comfort:

1. **Start Small:** Practice in low-pressure situations with friends or family. Hold eye contact briefly, then increase the duration as you grow comfortable.

2. **Mirror Their Gaze:** Match the gaze of your communication partner to show attentiveness and interest.

3. **Engage with Strangers:** Make brief eye contact with shopkeepers or passersby to build confidence in real-world settings.

4. **Reflect and Adjust:** Share your goals with trusted peers. Their feedback can help you refine your approach.

Consistency is key. Incorporate these exercises into your daily interactions to unlock the deeper connections meaningful eye contact creates.

Chapter Wrap-Up

As you refine your presentation skills, remember that eye contact is a powerful tool. It engages and captivates your audience, builds credibility, and fosters a deeper connection. By maintaining meaningful eye contact, you demonstrate confidence and sincerity, ensuring your message is both heard and felt. Practice and preparation will make eye contact feel natural and effective.

Next time you present, harness the power of eye contact to turn your presentations into compelling experiences that leave a lasting impact.

Chapter Thirty-four

The Art of Heart-to-Heart Connection: Lessons from Robert Fripp

Within the realms of progressive rock and inspirational speaking, few names resonate as profoundly as Robert Fripp's.[72] Known for his groundbreaking work with the legendary prog rock band King Crimson and as an eloquent keynote speaker, Fripp has left an indelible mark on the hearts and minds of many. Through my journey into Fripp's world—attending King Crimson concerts and hearing his speeches—I've discovered something profound. It's not merely about the music or the eloquence; it's about Fripp's unique ability to connect with his audiences on a deep level.

While emulating Fripp's virtuosic guitar skills may seem Herculean for most, what I uncovered is just as impactful and far more attainable. It's a skill within reach for anyone willing to learn.

Connection Beyond the Notes

Robert Fripp embodies many qualities that contribute to his success, both as a musician and a speaker. His expertise and dedication to his craft are immediately apparent, setting a high bar in both realms. However, beyond technical prowess and intricate compositions, Fripp imparts a profound lesson in engagement. It's not in the notes he plays, but, as he often says, *"in the spaces in between."* It's in the silent language of connection.

For those of us not blessed with the dexterity or musical genius akin to Fripp's, there exists a more essential skill that he demonstrates with virtuosity. One that we can all aspire to perfect: the art of making a heart-to-heart connection with our audience. This skill, potent in its simplicity, begins with the genuine act of making eye contact. Yet, Fripp elevates this act to a higher level, augmenting a simple gaze with a profound, sweeping gesture of heart-to-heart connection.

---

72. Musician, songwriter, record producer, and author, best known as the guitarist, founder and longest-lasting member of the progressive rock band King Crimson.

The Gesture of Heart Sweeping

At his concerts and keynotes, Fripp engages in a ritual that might at first glance seem like a simple scanning of the crowd. However, it is so much more. Instead of merely sweeping his eyes across the audience, he offers his heart. Fripp turns his whole body to make eye-to-eye and heart-to-heart contact with each person in the room, embodying a gesture that transcends visual contact. It's about creating a deeper, emotional engagement. This act, which I like to call "heart sweeping," is not about seeing; it's about feeling and connecting. It ensures that each person feels acknowledged, appreciated, and valued.

What makes this technique so powerful is its universal applicability. Unlike the years of practice required to achieve proficiency with a musical instrument, heart sweeping is an art that hinges on sincerity, empathy, and the willingness to connect deeply with others. It underscores the fact that genuine connections are not solely built on shared expertise or knowledge, but on the universal human experience of emotion and empathy.

Courage and Openness

Emulating Robert Fripp's heart-to-heart connection doesn't require musical talent, but it does demand courage and openness. It asks us to step beyond our comfort zones, to turn towards our audience—not just with our eyes, but with our entire being—and to offer our hearts in a silent, yet profoundly communicative gesture. This technique, simple in its execution, but deep in its impact, can transform the dynamics of interaction, whether on stage, in a concert venue, or in everyday encounters.

A Lesson for Our Times

In a world increasingly defined by superficial connections and digital interactions, the lesson of heart sweeping serves as a timely reminder of the power of genuine human connection. It may not teach you to play guitar like Robert Fripp—who in the world could? But it will guide you toward forging deeper, more meaningful relationships with those around you.

So, the next time you find yourself in front of an audience, remember Fripp's lesson: turn not only your gaze, but your heart towards those you wish to reach, and watch the magic of true connection unfold.

Action Steps:

1. **Practice Heart Sweeping**: Begin with a simple exercise of making eye contact with someone and focusing on how it feels to truly connect. Gradually expand this to larger groups.

2. **Engage with Empathy**: Approach each interaction with sincerity and a genuine desire to acknowledge and value others.

3. **Turn with Intention**: When addressing an audience, physically turn your body toward them to embody openness and connection.

4. **Start Small**: Try applying heart sweeping techniques in everyday encounters, such as meetings or conversations, to build comfort and skill.

5. **Reflect and Refine**: After each interaction, reflect on how you connected with others and consider ways to deepen that connection next time.

Chapter Thirty-five

Conversational Storytelling: The Secret to Deep Connection

Have you ever felt like a presenter was talking directly to you, even in a packed room? It's not just their words—it's the way they speak, as though letting you in on something personal, something profound. This is the magic of conversational storytelling.[73] It's not a method to memorize, but a mindset to embody, transforming presentations into memorable experiences.

Flipping the Script: From Performance to Conversation

Traditional presentations often feel like performances. The presenter delivers. The audience receives. But conversational storytelling[74] breaks down this barrier. It's not about dazzling a crowd with polished lines; it's about co-creating an experience.

Picture this: You're standing before a large audience, but instead of speaking to a crowd, you imagine a conversation with just one person—a friend, a colleague, or even yourself. Then, you extend that intimate connection to everyone in the room, responding to their unspoken thoughts, emotions, and expressions. Suddenly, everything shifts. The task feels less daunting, and the connection becomes deeply personal.

Start Small: Storytelling for One

Great storytelling starts with a single listener in mind. Craft your narrative as if you're speaking to one person—a representative of your audience. This isn't about simplification; it's about personalization.

---

73. Livia Polanyi. Telling the American Story: A Structural and Cultural Analysis of Conversational Storytelling. United States: Bloomsbury Academic, 1985.
74. M. Stelting, "Affectivity in Conversational Storytelling: An Analysis of Displays of Anger or Indignation in Complaint Stories." Pragmatics, 2, 2010. 229-277.

For example, instead of saying, *"Many people find this challenging,"* try asking, *"Have you ever faced this challenge?"* That subtle shift draws listeners in, making them feel seen. It's not a broadcast; it's a conversation. And when people feel included, they engage.

The Art of Pausing

Silence can be powerful. Pauses in a story allow your words to resonate, giving your audience space to think, laugh, or internalize. They're like punctuation in a conversation—essential for clarity and impact.

When you deliver a meaningful insight or share a personal anecdote, pause. Let your words breathe. Silence shows confidence in your message and respect for your audience, turning a one-sided presentation into a shared dialogue.

Why Conversational Storytelling Works

When you tell stories conversationally, you transform listeners from passive spectators into active participants. They're not just hearing you; they're feeling your story, reflecting on it, and connecting with it. It becomes a shared experience.

This approach also eases the pressure on you. Instead of striving for perfection in front of a crowd, you focus on building one connection at a time. The result? Authenticity. And authenticity is greater than perfection every time.

A New Way to Communicate

Conversational storytelling[75] is not about scripts or slides. It's a mindset—a way of reimagining communication. Your audience isn't a sea of anonymous faces; they're individuals, each with their own thoughts and feelings. When you shift your perspective, you don't just become a better presenter; you become a more empathetic one.

---

75. Monika Fludernik.. "Conversational Storytelling." In The Cambridge Companion to Narrative, edited by David Herman, 109–123. Cambridge: Cambridge University Press, 2007. https://www.cambridge.org/core/books/abs/cambridge-companion-to-narrative/conversational-storytelling/C83CB371A6DF426251DD40B602D93026.
Norrick, Neal R. Conversational Narrative: Storytelling in Everyday Talk. Amsterdam: John Benjamins Publishing Company, 2000. https://api.pageplace.de/preview/DT0400.9789027299550_A24762716/preview-9789027299550_A24762716.pdf.

Action Steps:

1. **Visualize One Listener**: Before your next presentation, imagine you're speaking to one person. Tailor your story to them, considering their perspective and challenges.

2. **Use Pauses**: Incorporate intentional pauses to let your audience reflect and connect with your message.

3. **Invite Interaction**: Welcome feedback, questions, or challenges. Treat these as opportunities to deepen the connection.

4. **Reflect and Refine**: After each presentation, evaluate what resonated and what didn't. Use these insights to continuously improve.

The Lasting Impact

Conversational storytelling isn't just a tool—it's a philosophy. It invites you to connect, inspire, and leave a lasting impression. Once you embrace it, you'll wonder how you ever communicated differently.

So, the next time you stand in front of an audience, don't just speak *to* them. Speak *with* them. Create a conversation that lingers in their minds long after the final word.

Chapter Thirty-six
Speak with Authority, Silence the Doubt

In your mind's eye, imagine you're sitting in the audience, waiting to be inspired. The presenter steps on stage, brimming with confidence. They begin, and for a moment, you're hooked—until it happens. "Uhm," they stammer, or perhaps, "ya know," and just like that, the spell breaks. Instead of absorbing their message, you're counting their verbal missteps.

Sound familiar? These credibility killers, known as disfluencies, are more than just annoying filler. They're a wrecking ball to authority, a distraction that pulls focus away from your ideas. If you've ever found yourself lost in the haze of a presenter's "likes" and "ah's," you know the damage these verbal ticks can do. But here's the truth: they're avoidable, and with practice, you can banish them entirely.

The Dance of Silence and Credibility

Disfluencies often creep in when our brains race ahead of our words, scrambling to fill the gaps. Ironically, the antidote isn't to speak faster or smoother, but to embrace the pause. Yes, silence is golden. (Cliché Alert!)

A pause isn't a failure to speak—it's a moment to think, to breathe, to connect. Picture it as the dramatic pause in a symphony. It commands attention, builds anticipation, and gives your words room to resonate. Silence doesn't diminish your message; it amplifies it. Replace the next "uhm" bubbling in your throat with a deep breath and see how the room leans in.

Consider how a well-placed pause transforms a sentence: *"Our team has seen... remarkable growth this year."* It exudes control, confidence, and thoughtfulness. Compare that to, *"Our team has seen... uh... remarkable growth, ya know?"* One word—one moment of hesitation—and your authority starts to crack.

Influence Amplified

Now let's look at two small words with big consequences: "so" and "and." These tiny connectors[76] can balloon your sentences into long-winded tangles that exhaust your audience. Consider this example: *"So, we'll take a break now, so, when we come back, we can start on time, and then we'll finish early, so you have time for your next meeting."* Exhausting, isn't it? Now imagine this instead: *"Let's take a break. When we return, we'll start on time and finish early. You'll have plenty of time for your next meeting."* The sentence is over. Buy a period. Start another one. Shorter sentences. Clearer message. Stronger impact!

The Power of Precision

Credibility extends beyond silencing disfluencies. It's about precision—getting your facts right and your delivery polished. Have you ever listened to a presenter misquote a source or stumble over a term? It's jarring. Suddenly, instead of focusing on their point, you're questioning their preparation. And when doubt creeps in, trust walks out. When that happens, the connection between us is broken.

I once gave a presentation to a group of grocery executives and mentioned that salsa has outsold ketchup in the U.S. since 1992. One of the executives, clearly skeptical, pulled out their phone to fact-check me. I paused and asked what they found. For a moment, the room held its breath. Thankfully, Google backed me up, and from that moment, I had the room's trust. If I'd been wrong, though, my credibility—and my message—would've crumbled.

Accuracy is non-negotiable. Check your facts. Attribute your sources. Missteps here don't just dent your credibility—they vaporize it.

Connection Through Humility

Even the most polished presenters stumble. The difference between losing credibility and gaining it often comes down to how you handle mistakes. The audience doesn't expect perfection; they expect honesty. If you slip, own it. Correct yourself. A simple, *"I misspoke,"* or *"Let me clarify,"* not only repairs trust but strengthens the connection between you and your audience.

---

76. Conjunctions to you grammar nerds.

Authenticity and humility are your secret weapons. People connect with presenters who come across as human, not robotic. Admitting an error shows you value the truth over your ego—and that's a credibility booster.

Building a Foundation of Trust

So how do you ensure your credibility stays intact? Preparation is the bedrock. Practice your delivery until your words flow naturally. Think of your ideas as building blocks. Share one thought, then pause. Share another, then pause again. By chunking your message, you eliminate the temptation to fill gaps with meaningless sounds and make your speech more deliberate. Record yourself, listen back, and identify where you falter. These steps aren't shortcuts—they're investments in trust.

But preparation isn't just about avoiding mistakes. It's about exuding confidence in every moment—confidence that invites the audience to trust you, to believe in your message.

Action Steps:

1. **Fact-Check:** Before any presentation, review your content to ensure every statistic, quote, or claim is accurate and up-to-date.

2. **Credit Your Sources:** Practice giving proper attribution in your presentation. Highlighting credible sources reinforces your own credibility.

3. **Rehearse for Confidence:** Spend time rehearsing your delivery to minimize errors, disfluencies, and missteps.

4. **Prepare for Skeptics:** Anticipate questions or challenges from your audience and have evidence ready to back up your claims.

5. **Embrace Transparency:** If you're unsure about something during your presentation, admit it. Transparency builds trust far more than pretending to know everything.

6. **Practice Silence:** Train yourself to pause instead of using fillers. Silence is a powerful tool that conveys confidence and authority.

7. **Chunk Your Ideas:** Break your content into clear, digestible segments to make your message deliberate and impactful.

Chapter Wrap-up

Every word you say, every pause you hold, and every fact you share reflects your credibility. Trust is fragile. Nurture it by speaking with authority, embracing silence, and preparing with care. Your audience isn't just listening—they're deciding. Will they follow your lead or tune you out? The choice lies in your ability to speak with precision and poise.

Chapter Thirty-seven

Big Stage, Small Screen: Tailoring Your Presentation to the Medium

Imagine walking onto a grand stage. The lights are bright, the audience waits, and every seat—from the front row to the last—is filled with expectant faces. In this moment, your voice, gestures, and energy must expand to fill the entire space. Now, compare this to stepping in front of a camera for a virtual meeting. There's no stage, little immediate feedback, and your presentation is confined to the size of a screen. Each medium demands something different, just like how an actor shifts between performing on stage and acting for film. The key to success? Knowing when to amplify and when to rein it in.

Project Like You're on Broadway

When presenting in person, think of yourself as a Broadway performer. Every element—your voice, gestures, expressions—must reach the farthest corner of the room. Your energy isn't just for the front row; it's for the person sitting in the last seat who needs to feel as connected to your message as those up front.

Grand gestures and a powerful voice are your tools. Amplifying emotions is essential to ensure your audience experiences the full depth of your message. You need to broadcast your presence across the room, much like a theater actor who becomes 'larger than life.' Still, it's not about becoming a caricature. It's about being the most expansive, authentic version of yourself.

In this in-person setting, there's an immediacy. You're sharing a moment in real-time, with no filter between you and your audience. Your movements, tone, and expressions need to engage them and create an immersive experience. But if you tried this same approach on camera? It would overwhelm and feel out of place. Which leads us to the next medium: the screen.

Influence Amplified

Zoom or Teams: The Intimacy of the Camera

When presenting virtually or recording for later playback, the stage fades away, replaced by the close, personal lens of a camera. Here, your audience is only a foot-and-a-half away from your face. The grand gestures you used on stage now seem exaggerated. Just as a television actor adapts to the camera's magnification of every subtle expression, so must you.

In a virtual setting, your audience sees every small shift in your eyes, every flicker of emotion. Your gestures shrink, your voice softens, and instead of projecting to fill a room, you focus on creating a connection within the small, intimate frame. Think of it as controlled energy.

A close analogy is television acting. Actors don't perform for the camera or even into the camera; they perform with their scene partners, which the camera captures. On Zoom, Teams, or any virtual platform, your goal is to connect—not perform for the camera itself, but for the people on the other end of it. To keep things natural and authentic, focus on nuanced expressions, balanced tone, and controlled gestures.

Striking the Right Balance

How do you know when to "go big" and when to hold back? It's about refining your sense of balance, much like an actor adjusting between stage and screen performance. Presenting in person is about expansion—bringing energy outward to fill the room. Presenting virtually is about precision—focusing energy inward to connect through the camera.

Personally, I prefer in-person presentations. There's something dynamic about interacting directly with an audience. It's akin to "breaking the fourth wall"[77] in theater—when an actor acknowledges the audience, engaging with them directly. In an in-person presentation, the audience isn't just there to listen; they are active participants in the experience, often co-creators of the energy in the room.

---

77. In the theater world, to "break the fourth wall" is to disrupt the imaginary barrier between performers and the audience, typically by directly acknowledging or addressing them, thus breaking the illusion of the fictional world.

In contrast, presenting virtually can feel disconnected, as if there's that fourth wall between you and the audience. The camera serves as the intermediary. It's not about which format is better; it's about adapting your approach to suit each medium. Just as a Broadway actor might relish the immediate feedback from a live audience, a television actor appreciates the intimacy the camera captures.

Adapting to the Medium: Practical Tips

1. **For the Stage:** Use your entire body. Your gestures need to be large enough for everyone to see, but still purposeful. Don't just wave your hands for effect—every movement should support your message. Stand tall, project your voice, and make sure your energy radiates to every corner of the room.

2. **For the Screen:** Scale it back. Focus on facial expressions and smaller hand movements. Speak clearly, but there's no need to project—your audience is much closer to you. Remember, they can see every nuance, so be mindful of your facial expressions and make eye contact with the camera, not the thumbnails on your screen.

3. **Energy Management:** In-person presentations often require bursts of high energy to keep the audience engaged. On camera, sustained energy is key, though it's subtler. In both cases, stay aware of your pacing, and don't let adrenaline dictate your performance.

4. **Engagement:** In person, you can read the room *(page 66)* and adjust on the fly based on audience reactions. On camera, engaging your audience requires a more deliberate approach. Ask questions, invite participation, and don't shy away from silences—they give people time to process what you're saying.

5. **Preparation:** Regardless of the medium, preparation is critical. For in-person events, practice projecting your voice and incorporating purposeful movements. For virtual presentations, rehearse in front of a camera. Watch the playback to check your body language and expressions. Adapt accordingly.

That's a Wrap

Adapting your presentation style to the medium isn't just about technical tweaks—it's about mindset. Much like how an actor transports an audience into a world of make-believe, your job as a presenter is to create meaningful connections, no matter the setting. Understanding when to go big and when to be more restrained is the key to tailoring your delivery.

By thinking of yourself as both a Broadway performer and a television actor, you'll ensure that no matter the medium, your message resonates and connects. The magic lies in knowing how to adapt—not just your words, but your energy, movements, and presence. Whether on a big stage or a small screen, tailoring your approach invites your audience into the heart of your message, no matter where they are.

Chapter Thirty-eight
Secrets for Executives to Shine

Imagine stepping onto a stage, the room buzzing with anticipation. Your slides are ready, your material practiced, and then—the microphone cuts out. Or perhaps, halfway through, an audience member's unexpected question derails your flow. These moments can feel like disasters. But they're not. They're opportunities—chances to show your composure, adaptability, and most importantly, your humanity. Excelling in the art of speaking is about more than preparation; it's about owning the stage, connecting with your audience, and staying agile no matter what comes your way.

The Foundation of Confidence

1. Own Your Presence

Your presence in front of a group is your silent introduction. Confidence starts with how you carry yourself. Remember the neutral stance? Stand tall, shoulders back, feet shoulder-width apart, and arms relaxed at your sides. Every movement should project authority. Think of your body as a visual aid that's always on display. Intentional gestures, purposeful movement, and controlled expressions can enhance your message as much as your words. When you look the part of a leader, people are more likely to trust your message.

2. Tap Into Your Authenticity

Audiences crave authenticity. Forget trying to mimic another presenter or adopting a persona that isn't you. Instead, lean into your natural style and personality. Authenticity builds trust, and trust amplifies influence. This doesn't mean winging it; preparation is key. Know your material so well that you can adapt to audience reactions while staying true to your message. Think of your presentation as a conversation, not a monologue.

3. Boost the Art of Breathing

Most people don't think about their breathing until they're nervous—and then it betrays them. Shallow, rapid breaths can make you sound anxious and diminish your vocal power. Diaphragmatic breathing, or "belly breathing," creates a strong, resonant voice and calms your nerves. It's the foundation of vocal confidence.

Here's how to practice it:

- **Get Comfortable**: Assume a neutral stance. Place one hand on your chest and the other on your abdomen.
- **Inhale Deeply**: Breathe in slowly through your nose, feeling your abdomen rise as your diaphragm expands. Your chest should stay still.
- **Exhale Fully**: Breathe out gently through your mouth, feeling your abdomen fall.
- **Repeat**: Practice for 5–10 minutes, focusing on slow, controlled breaths.

Not only will this strengthen your voice, but it will also help you feel grounded and in control.

Agility in Action: The Art of Improvisation

4. The Mindset: "Yes, and..."

Borrow a key principle from improv theater: the "Yes, and... "[78] mindset. When something unexpected happens—whether it's a technical glitch or an off-topic question—acknowledge it (Yes) and build on it constructively (and...). For example, if your slides fail mid-presentation, say, *"Looks like technology wants to test my storytelling skills today. Let's roll with it!"* This not only diffuses tension, but also demonstrates your ability to handle pressure with grace.

---

78. The phrase *"Yes, and..."* comes from the principles of improvisational theater. It was introduced by Viola Spolin, known as the "mother of improvisation," and expanded by her son Paul Sills and the performers at The Second City in Chicago. Del Close, another key figure in improv, popularized it as a core technique for fostering collaboration during his work with The Second City and IO Theater (formerly ImprovOlympic).

Improvisation skills help you adapt to questions, challenges, or unexpected moments. Engage your audience by soliciting their input or reactions. For example, if a tough question arises, say, *"Great question. Let's hear how others in the room might approach this."* This creates collaboration and buys you time to formulate a thoughtful response.

When disruptions occur, pretending they don't exist only creates tension. Instead, call them out. If an audience member asks an off-topic question, recognize it graciously: *"That's an interesting angle. Let's explore it briefly before we tie it back to today's focus."* Addressing the moment demonstrates confidence and keeps the energy flowing.

5. Practice Structured Flexibility

Plan your presentation in modules that can be reordered or skipped without losing coherence. This way, if time is cut short or audience interest shifts, you can adapt seamlessly. Think of your content as building blocks you can rearrange on the fly.

6. Command the Space

How you move on stage communicates as much as your words. Avoid pacing aimlessly or standing rigidly. Step forward to emphasize a point. Move laterally to engage different parts of the room. Use purposeful gestures to draw your audience in. Each movement should reinforce your message.

Connection Over Perfection

7. Engage Through Vocal Dynamics

A monotone voice can lull even the most attentive audience into boredom. Vary your pitch, power (volume), and pace to keep listeners engaged. *(see Chapter Thirty-two)* Pauses, when used effectively, can emphasize key points and give your audience time to absorb your message. Your voice is an instrument—play it well to reflect your passion and conviction.

8. Harness the Power of Storytelling

Stories humanize your message and create emotional bonds. Share anecdotes that illustrate your points, and don't shy away from vulnerability. When done right, storytelling transforms dry data into memorable narratives that resonate.

9. Reading the Room

Your audience is your greatest asset when navigating unpredictability. Watch for cues like body language or facial expressions. If they seem disengaged, pivot to a story or interactive exercise. If their energy spikes around a particular topic, expand on it. Staying attuned to their reactions keeps your presentation dynamic and relevant.

10. Focus on Connection, Not Perfection

Audiences connect with people, not perfection. Don't stress about flawless slides or memorizing every word. Be present in the moment, listen to the energy of the room, and adjust accordingly. This shows your audience that you value their time and input.

Building Resilience and Leaving an Impression

11. Build Emotional Resilience

Stay calm under pressure. When disruptions occur, take a deep breath and reframe nerves as excitement. This pause not only centers you, but also reassures your audience. Agility isn't just about quick thinking; it's about emotional control.

12. Simplify Under Pressure

When caught off guard, resist the urge to overcomplicate. Focus on one clear idea that ties back to your core message. Clarity and brevity will help you regain control and keep your audience engaged.

13. Practice, but Perform Naturally

Preparation breeds confidence, but performance requires spontaneity. Rehearse until you know your material inside out. Then, let it go. On stage, focus on engaging your audience, not reciting your script. This balance between preparation and presence is what sets exceptional presenters apart.

14. Leave a Lasting Impression

Your closing moments are your audience's takeaway. Make them count. Whether it's a powerful call to action, a compelling story, or a resonant phrase, ensure your finale reinforces your message and leaves your audience inspired.

Action Steps:

1. **Refine Your Presence**: Practice standing tall and moving purposefully to project confidence.

2. **Discover Your Authentic Voice**: Reflect on your unique style and deliver your message with genuine passion.

3. **Strengthen Your Breathing**: Incorporate diaphragmatic breathing into your routine to improve vocal control.

4. **Experiment with Vocal Variety**: Record yourself practicing vocal dynamics and seek feedback.

5. **Weave Stories Into Your Presentation**: Identify anecdotes that illustrate key points and practice integrating them.

6. **Improve Improvisation**: Engage in exercises to build flexibility and confidence.

7. **Engage Your Audience**: Focus on connection through eye contact, movement, and active listening.

8. **Close With Impact**: Rehearse a powerful ending that reinforces your message and leaves a lasting impression.

Unpredictable speaking situations aren't pitfalls—they're platforms to showcase your adaptability and connection with your audience. With these strategies, you'll be ready to step onto any stage and make your mark.

Chapter Thirty-nine

Set the Stage for Success: Why Your Presentation Depends on More Than Just Content & Delivery

You've spent weeks crafting your presentation and perfecting your delivery. Though, no matter how strong your content is, success depends on more than what you say. It also relies on how well the technical and environmental elements support your message. While the AV team can't improve your content, they can definitely harm it if things go wrong. Every detail—sound, lighting, and visuals—needs to align with your needs. Preparation is key. Let's look at the factors that can make or break your presentation beyond the content itself.

The Role of the AV Team

The AV team ensures your presentation's technical foundation—sound, visuals, and lighting—runs smoothly. While they won't elevate your message, technical issues can certainly weaken it. Imagine the microphone crackling or the lighting casting shadows on your face. Instead of focusing on you, the audience gets distracted by the glitches, undermining your message.

Take Ownership of AV Setup

Don't assume the AV setup will be perfect when you arrive. Take responsibility to ensure it fits your presentation style. Test the equipment ahead of time. Adjust the lighting, microphone levels, and sound to suit your needs. Proactive checks prevent surprises and ensure a smooth delivery.

Audio and Visual Quality: Essentials for Engagement

Clear sound and sharp visuals are fundamental. Your voice is your primary tool, and sound clarity keeps the audience engaged. A quick sound check can prevent issues like microphone feedback or volume drops. Similarly, make sure your visuals are crisp. Dim projectors or blurry images dilute the impact of your slides or videos. Quality audio and visuals keep the audience focused on your message.

Avoiding Technical Disruptions

Nothing derails a presentation faster than technical glitches. A malfunctioning clicker, delayed video, or frozen slides interrupt your flow and shift your focus from the message to fixing the problem. These mishaps break your connection with the audience. To avoid them, test all equipment, from the microphone to the clicker, in advance.

Room Layout and Stage Setup: Engage with Ease

Room arrangement affects how you engage with the audience. The seating setup—whether theater-style, classroom, boardroom, u-shaped or banquet tables—and the location of aisles shape how easily you can connect. Ensure sightlines are clear, and the layout supports interaction. A well-arranged room fosters rapport and keeps attention on you.

Command the Room with Stage Positioning

Your stage placement impacts how you connect with the audience. Too far back, and you create distance; too close, and it overwhelms the front row. Ideally, the stage should allow you to command the room while staying approachable. Make sure you have enough space to move if needed, and ensure the steps or access points are safe.

Screen Placement: Maximizing Visibility and Impact

Effective screen placement ensures every audience member can clearly see your visuals without obstruction, enhancing engagement and focus. Avoid relying on a single screen directly behind you or at the center of the stage, as your movement may block the view. Instead, position screens to the sides of the stage or use multiple screens distributed throughout the room for unobstructed visibility.

Strategic placement also allows you to move freely across the stage without worrying about standing in front of your visuals. This keeps the stage clear and fosters a stronger connection with your audience, as you can engage directly while ensuring your visuals are accessible to everyone in the room.

Lighting: Stay in the Spotlight

Good lighting can elevate your presentation, while poor lighting can diminish it. Dim or harsh lights can obscure your presence, while good lighting highlights you and your visuals. Adjust the lighting to suit your style, whether you need soft ambiance or bright spotlights. If natural light is a factor, test how it affects visibility throughout the day.

Preparation is Key: Don't Leave It to Chance

Even the best content can falter if the technical setup or room arrangement isn't right. A pre-presentation walk-through is essential. Test the AV equipment, check the layout, and ensure the lighting works from different audience perspectives. If something feels off, ask for adjustments. Small tweaks can significantly improve your connection with the audience.

Test, Verify, Adjust

To ensure a seamless presentation, test every detail. Walk through the room, check the sightlines, and verify that sound and lighting are in sync with your content. Taking the time to test and adjust guarantees everything runs smoothly.

Chapter Wrap-up: Setting Yourself Up for Success

A successful presentation isn't just about great content—it's about creating an environment where every element supports you. The AV team may not enhance your message, but technical issues can definitely detract from it. By testing and adjusting the AV setup, room layout, stage and screen placement, and lighting, you create an atmosphere that amplifies your message. Preparation is your best tool to ensure success from start to finish.

Action Steps:

1. **Schedule a Walkthrough:** Arrange to visit the presentation venue beforehand to familiarize yourself with the room layout, stage, and AV setup.

2. **Test Equipment Early:** Arrive early to test microphones, projectors, clickers, and other technical equipment. Address any issues before your presentation begins.

3. **Optimize Lighting:** Work with the AV team to ensure lighting highlights you without creating harsh shadows or diminishing visibility.

4. **Check Sightlines:** Walk the room to confirm that every audience member will have a clear view of the stage and screens.

5. **Rehearse with Equipment:** Practice your presentation using the venue's equipment to ensure a seamless integration of your content and delivery.

6. **Communicate Needs Clearly:** Provide the AV team with specific instructions about your preferences for sound, lighting, and screen placement.

7. **Bring Backup Tools:** Carry extra batteries, adapters, and a second copy of your presentation on a USB drive or cloud storage.

8. **Stay Flexible:** Be prepared to adapt to last-minute changes in room setup or technical challenges.

9. **Engage the AV Team:** Build a rapport with the AV staff. Their support can make a significant difference in handling unforeseen issues.

10. **Review and Reflect:** After your presentation, take notes on what worked and what could be improved for future events.

Part Eight
Lessons from the Stage

Every venue, whether it's a conference hall, a corporate boardroom, or a virtual meeting, teaches its own lessons. The moments of triumph and challenge, the unexpected audience reactions, and the inevitable adjustments shape not just your presentation, but your presence as a communicator. This section dives into the real-world insights gained from stepping onto the stage—what works, what doesn't, and how to adapt when things don't go as planned.

From navigating audience interaction to conquering stage fright, these chapters reveal the art of learning on your feet. They show how every experience, whether it's a perfectly executed presentation or an on-the-fly adjustment, sharpens your ability to engage and connect. Through practical strategies and reflections, you'll learn how to turn every presentation into a powerful lesson in leadership and adaptability. These lessons aren't just about surviving the stage—they're about thriving on it.

Chapter Forty

Crafting a TED-Worthy Talk: Insights from My Journey

What makes a TED talk stick—not just with the audience in the moment, but in their minds long after the applause fades? After directing six TEDx events and coaching countless speakers, I've uncovered the essential ingredients. Creating a TED-worthy talk isn't just about dazzling delivery; it's about crafting an idea that captivates and resonates deeply. Let's explore how you can do just that.

Identifying the Idea

A TED talk's foundation is its message. TEDx committees don't chase fame; they seek brilliance. A powerful idea shines brighter than a big name.

Keep it simple. TED talks succeed because they focus on one clear idea—an idea that's easy to grasp, yet profoundly impactful. Choose a topic that resonates with you and connects deeply with your audience.

Go deep, not wide. Instead of skimming the surface, guide your audience into the depths of your idea's 'how' and 'why.' A TED talk isn't about handing out answers; it's about taking your audience on a journey of discovery.

Be fresh, credible, and surprising. Avoid rehashing old TED content. If your topic isn't entirely new, frame it in an unexpected way. Originality sets you apart. Ground your idea in reality by sharing its potential to make an impact, even if it's still in its early stages.

Start close to home. Ideas that directly impact local communities often resonate most deeply. The best TEDx talks challenge the status quo and offer fresh perspectives that inspire change.

Expanding the Idea

Lay the groundwork. Build your message on familiar concepts so your audience can follow along easily. Analogies and relatable stories are your secret weapons; they make your message memorable and your idea accessible.

Harness the power of storytelling. Stories captivate. A well-crafted narrative guides your audience, weaving your idea into personal anecdotes and relatable experiences.

Use visuals strategically. Visual aids should complement your words, not overshadow them. A striking image or meaningful graphic can make your idea stick.

Keep it accessible. Even if your audience is familiar with the subject, break down complex topics into digestible, relatable pieces.

Engaging the Audience

Shift perspectives. Offer a new lens—one that refocuses their view and sparks a desire for change.

Make them care. Connect emotionally. Show your audience why your idea matters and how it impacts their lives. Emotional connections build engagement and drive action.

Invite critical thinking. Frame your idea to inspire conversations and exploration. Leave room for reflection and curiosity.

Structuring the Presentation

Create a clear path. Your presentation should flow like a well-marked trail, leading to a powerful conclusion. Start strong, build momentum, and finish with impact.

Inspire sharing. A TED talk is meant to spread. Make your idea novel, useful, and shareable, extending its reach beyond the event.

Execution

Rehearse relentlessly. Practice until your delivery is seamless. Seek feedback from trusted colleagues or mentors, and refine your presentation until it's sharp and polished.

Speak with authenticity. Let your passion shine. Your sincerity and energy will electrify your words and amplify your message.

Tips for All Presentations

- **Passion and Authenticity:** Genuine enthusiasm resonates and builds trust.
- **Hot Opening:** Start with a surprising fact, provocative question, or compelling anecdote.
- **Conversational Style:** Speak naturally. Build rapport through relatability.
- **Jaw-Dropping Moments:** Add moments of surprise that delight and engage.
- **Emotional Appeal:** Use humor, empathy, or inspiration to evoke emotions.
- **Supportive Visuals:** Enhance understanding without distracting from your message.
- **Simple and Clear Messages:** Keep your core idea straightforward and easy to grasp.
- **Strong Conclusion:** End with a memorable takeaway and a call to action.

Chapter Wrap-Up

By embracing these strategies, you'll craft a TEDx talk that doesn't just inform—it transforms. Whether your aim is to spark change locally or make a global impact, your presentation can leave a lasting legacy.

Remember, the journey to the red dot is as important as the talk itself. Build a monument with your words—one that stands tall long after the applause fades.

Action Steps:

1. **Identify Your Idea:** Write down your core message. Is it clear, fresh, and meaningful?

2. **Refine Your Story:** Develop a narrative that connects emotionally and logically.

3. **Test Your Talk:** Share your idea with a small group for feedback.

4. **Rehearse with Purpose:** Practice your delivery to ensure it's authentic and polished.

5. **Design Visuals Wisely:** Choose images or graphics that enhance understanding.

6. **Engage Emotionally:** Consider how your idea impacts your audience and address their needs directly.

Chapter Forty-one

The Three Speeches: Lessons from the Keynote Stage

There's a saying about presenting that anyone who's been on stage can relate to: there are three speeches—the one you planned to give, the one you gave, and the one you wished you gave. This insightful observation, often attributed to Dale Carnegie,[79] perfectly captures the unpredictable nature of presenting, especially when the stakes are high. It also reflects the gap between intention and execution—a gap that every presenter must learn to navigate.

The Speech I Planned to Give

My approach was clear: craft a customerized *(see page 71)* keynote for a room full of executives from the same industry. The theme? AI: The Future is Now. The client needed a one-hour presentation that was both impactful and tailored specifically for this audience. I prepared 56 minutes of material, meticulously designed to fit the time slot, leaving 4 minutes to spare.

The plan included a structured, section-by-section breakdown that would allow me to keep the session flowing smoothly. Audience interaction was built into the schedule, with a separate Q&A session planned afterward. Everything was prepared with the precision that comes from years of experience. But as any seasoned presenter knows, no speech survives first contact with the audience.[80]

Von Moltke's timeless wisdom—that plans rarely survive reality—is particularly relevant in speaking. Planning is essential, but flexibility and adaptability are critical when the unexpected inevitably arises.

---

[79]. Dale Carnegie, <u>Public Speaking and Influencing Men in Business</u>. United States: Association Press. 1946
[80]. Paraphrasing "No plan survives first contact with the enemy." Attributed to Helmuth von Moltke the Elder, a Prussian military strategist.

The Speech I Gave

From the very first question, the audience proved far more interactive than I'd anticipated. They weren't just listening passively; they were engaged, responding to prompts, and sharing thoughtful, concise examples. Imagine two microphone runners hustling to keep up with the flood of input. These executives weren't just attendees; they became co-creators of the keynote, shaping the conversation in real time.

At one point, I managed to speak with the client during a small-group discussion. *"I'm behind,"* I confessed, overwhelmed by the back-and-forth interaction. Her response? *"Keep going. The interaction is fantastic."* For any presenter, that's music to the ears. A captivated, engaged audience is the holy grail of speaking.

But here was the challenge: I was still up against a hard stop. I had to cut sections on the fly—a task made easier by my presentation's modular design *(see page 41)*. I compressed material, skipped topics, and made real-time decisions. Despite these adjustments, my carefully planned 56-minute keynote stretched to 100 minutes. I had committed the cardinal sin of professional speaking: going over time.

Yet, the client was thrilled. They understood the situation and appreciated the rich interaction. The audience's energy and engagement turned the session into something far greater than I could have ever planned.

The Speech I Wished I Gave

Reflection is crucial after any presentation. Looking back, I realized I underestimated how much this audience would want to participate. People no longer want to sit quietly and absorb information; they want to engage, question, and contribute. They crave a dialogue, not a monologue.

Knowing this, I could've prepared less material and left more room for improvisation. It's always easier to add detail if time allows than to cut sections under pressure. By embracing flexibility and the possibility of audience-led moments, I could've created an even more seamless experience.

Next time, I'll plan for the unexpected. Instead of building a rigid structure, I'll design a framework that allows room for the audience to shape the narrative.

The Takeaway

The concept of three speeches—the one you planned, the one you gave, and the one you wished you gave—is more than a clever phrase. It's a reality every presenter faces. The best way to prepare is to leave space for the unexpected and to recognize that your audience isn't just listening; they're participating.

Whether you're addressing a room full of executives or delivering a TEDx talk, it's not just about crafting the perfect presentation. It's about being ready to adapt, to listen, and to evolve your message in the moment. Ultimately, the best presentation might not be the one you imagined, but the one your audience helps you create.

Action Steps:

1. **Anticipate Interaction**: Build flexibility into your presentation by assembling it from modules that can be expanded or compressed based on audience engagement.
2. **Engage Early**: Start with a question or prompt to gauge your audience's energy and willingness to participate.
3. **Simplify Your Content**: Prepare less material and allow space for organic interaction. You don't have to tell them everything you know, just everything they need to know.[81]
4. **Practice Adaptability**: Rehearse adjusting your delivery in response to audience feedback.
5. **Reflect and Learn**: After every presentation, take time to evaluate what worked, what didn't, and what could be improved for next time.

---

81. An often-shared piece of advice emphasizing the importance of tailoring information to the audience's needs, focusing on what is most relevant and impactful rather than overwhelming them with excessive details.

Chapter Forty-two

Conquer Stage Fright with These Simple Tricks

How often has this happened to you: you're about to step on stage. Your palms are sweaty, your heart races, and rapid thoughts bounce around in your head: *What if I forget my words? What if I lose the audience? What if I embarrass myself?* Stage fright can feel like a mental battleground, with the spotlight amplifying your fears. It's no wonder speaking in front of people is consistently ranked as one of the greatest anxieties. But here's the twist—your fear isn't just about speaking. It's rooted in something deeper.

Stage fright often stems from fears of failure, rejection, and looking foolish. You're not just worried about the act of speaking; you're concerned your message won't land, that you'll forget your lines, or that the audience won't be impressed. These fears create a mental barrier that can feel insurmountable. The good news? You don't need to be fearless to conquer stage fright. You just need to shift your focus.

Here's the key shift: **it's not about you.**

Think about that. Your speech or presentation is never about you. It's about your audience. When you stop obsessing over your performance and start focusing on what your audience needs from your message, the anxiety starts to loosen its grip. The pressure to be perfect fades when you realize your job isn't to dazzle them with flawlessness. Your job is to connect, offer value, and share something meaningful. This mindset shift from self-focus to audience-focus can change everything.

Of course, changing your mindset is just part of the solution. Let's explore practical strategies that tackle stage fright from multiple angles.

1. Preparation and Practice

Preparation is your best defense against stage fright. The more you practice, the more confident you'll feel. But it's not just about memorizing your presentation—it's about understanding your content inside and out so you can speak naturally. Rehearse in front of friends or record yourself. The better you know your material, the less room there is for fear to creep in.

2. Breathing and Mindfulness Techniques

Stage fright often triggers your body's fight-or-flight response: rapid heartbeat, shallow breathing, and tense muscles. Deep breathing exercises can help calm these physical symptoms. Before stepping on stage, take a few slow, deep breaths to center yourself. Pair this with mindfulness techniques by focusing on the present moment rather than worrying about what might go wrong. This keeps your mind clear and reduces stress.

3. Visualize Success

Forget the outdated advice about picturing your audience in their underwear. Instead, try positive visualization. Imagine yourself delivering your presentation confidently, with the audience fully engaged. This mental rehearsal primes your brain for success, making you feel more at ease when the time comes.

4. Start Small, Build Confidence

Presenting in front of a large crowd can feel overwhelming, so start with smaller groups. Gradually build your confidence by speaking in familiar settings or to people you know. Each successful experience becomes a reference point, helping reduce your fear when the stakes are higher.

5. Nail Your Opening

Nerves tend to peak at the beginning of a presentation. That's why having a strong, well-practiced opening is crucial. Once you've nailed the first few minutes, your nerves start to subside, allowing you to settle into your delivery. A solid start sets the tone and boosts your confidence.

6. Embrace Imperfection

It's natural to fear making mistakes, but perfection isn't the goal. Audiences are more forgiving than you think, and a minor stumble can even make you more relatable. Trying to be flawless adds unnecessary pressure. Focus on connecting with your audience instead. They're not there to judge—they're there to listen.

7. Reframe Nervousness as Excitement

Did you know the physical symptoms of nervousness are nearly identical to those of excitement? The next time you feel your heart racing or your palms sweating, try reframing those feelings as excitement. This mental shift can turn nervous energy into enthusiasm, helping you channel it into a dynamic delivery.

8. Meet Your Audience Beforehand

One of the most underrated strategies to overcome stage fright is meeting a few audience members before stepping on stage. When you're about to present to a room full of strangers, the pressure can feel overwhelming. You might imagine worst-case scenarios: *What are they thinking? Will they be critical?* But when you take time to connect with a few people beforehand, the dynamic changes.

Instead of addressing a crowd of unknown faces, you're speaking to individuals you've already met. A quick handshake, a smile, or even a brief conversation helps humanize the audience. Suddenly, they're not a sea of judgment—they're just people. This rapport eases anxiety and makes the experience feel more natural. Plus, chatting with your audience beforehand gives you valuable insights into their interests and expectations, allowing you to tailor your message to resonate more deeply. Knowing you're delivering something meaningful boosts your confidence and calms the fear of falling short.

The Takeaway

By combining these techniques with the mindset shift of focusing on your audience, stage fright can be gradually diminished. It's about preparation, perspective, and practice. And remember, the goal isn't delivering a flawless performance. It's sharing your message in a way that connects with those in front of you. Focus on that, and watch your fear fade.

Action Steps:

1. **Practice Regularly:** Rehearse your presentation until you feel comfortable with the material.

2. **Use Deep Breathing:** Incorporate calming exercises to manage physical symptoms of stage fright.

3. **Visualize Success:** Spend time imagining a confident delivery and engaged audience.

4. **Start Small:** Build your speaking confidence by presenting to smaller groups.

5. **Prepare a Strong Opening:** Craft and rehearse an impactful introduction to set the tone.

6. **Reframe Nervousness:** Channel your energy into excitement rather than fear.

7. **Engage Beforehand:** Meet a few audience members to establish rapport and ease nerves.

Part Nine
Practice and Preparation

Great speeches aren't born on the stage; they're crafted long before the audience takes their seats. Every impactful presentation is the result of countless hours of practice, purposeful preparation, and the willingness to refine over and over again. In this section, we'll explore the transformative process that elevates good presenters into great communicators.

Through stories and lessons drawn from real-world experiences, these chapters reveal the art of deliberate practice and the unexpected parallels between crafting a presentation and overcoming life's challenges. You'll learn how preparation shapes your confidence, how rehearsal uncovers opportunities for growth, and why embracing imperfection is a powerful step toward continuous improvement. Whether you're preparing for a keynote or leading a team meeting, the lessons in this section will equip you to approach every speaking opportunity with intention, clarity, and an unshakable presence.

Chapter Forty-three

The Art and Science of Deliberate Practice: Elevating Your Professional Game

When you step onto a stage, the spotlight doesn't automatically elevate you to greatness. Instead, you fall to the level of your preparation.[82] This fundamental truth links the quality of your presentation to the effort invested in practice. Let's unpack what it means to practice effectively, focusing on the skills of Executive Presence and storytelling. These aren't magical abilities reserved for a select few; they're forged through deliberate, purposeful practice.[83]

The popular "10,000 Hour Rule"[84] suggests that sheer volume of practice creates expertise. But time alone isn't enough. Quality outweighs quantity. It's not about logging hours; it's about making those hours count.

Deliberate practice isn't aimless repetition. It's a structured effort, intentionally designed to improve performance. This method involves targeted goals, consistent feedback, and the guidance of skilled mentors who can provide immediate, actionable critiques. The old adage, *"Practice makes perfect,"* oversimplifies the process. In truth, *"Practice makes permanent."* Repeat mistakes without correction, and you're not heading toward excellence—you're cementing bad habits. Deliberate practice pushes beyond comfort zones, rectifies errors, and fosters meaningful growth.

---

82. This paraphrase of a quote frequently credited to an anonymous Navy Seal, is based on a quote from Greek philosopher Archilochus, "We don't rise to the level of our expectations; we fall to the level of our training."
83. K. Anders Ericsson, Ralf Th. Krampe, and Clemens Tesch-Romer, "The Role of Deliberate Practice in the Acquisition of Expert Performance" Psychological Review 1993, Vol. 100. No. 3, 363-406
84. Ibid.

Experts such as K. Anders Ericsson, the pioneer behind the deliberate practice framework,[85] and Daniel Goleman,[86] renowned for his work on emotional intelligence, emphasize the transformative power of precise feedback and expert guidance. Consider elite athletes: their coaches dissect every movement, offering tailored advice to refine technique. In the same way, achieving professional excellence demands that level of scrutiny and support.

This approach is equally transformative for storytelling and Executive Presence. The more you tell your stories, the more opportunities you create for feedback and refinement. Over time, these iterations allow you to capture attention and deliver messages with greater clarity and impact.

It's important to distinguish between practice and rehearsal. Practice hones specific skills, like crafting a compelling narrative or refining your delivery. Rehearsal, on the other hand, brings everything together. Emmy-nominated actor Donald Pleasence and Oscar-winning actor Michael Caine understood this distinction well. They noted that preparation culminates in rehearsals, where you see your work come to life. For many, rehearsal is the first time they hear their words out loud, revealing nuances and opportunities for improvement. As Caine aptly put it, *"By the time you get to the performance, you should be so familiar with what you are doing that it seems effortless."*[87]

> *"Rehearsals are where the magic happens. Rehearsals are where the growth happens. Rehearsals are where the learning happens."*[88]

They're the crucible for growth and learning, turning raw preparation into polished performance. This principle extends beyond the arts. In the corporate world, deliberate practice and rehearsal can elevate presentations, negotiations, and leadership moments to new heights.

---

85. Anders Ericsson and Robert Pool. Ericsson, Anders., Pool, Robert. Peak: Secrets from the New Science of Expertise. United States: Mariner Books/Houghton Mifflin Harcourt, 2017. Page 111
86. Goleman, Daniel. Focus: The Hidden Driver of Excellence. United Kingdom: HarperCollins, 2013.
87. Michael Caine. Blowing the Bloody Doors Off: And Other Lessons in Life. United States: Hachette Books, 2018. Chapter 6.
88. Paul Buyer, Drumline Gold: With Interviews by Aungst, Bachman, Daniels, Davila, DeLucia, Flum, Hannum, Henley, Kuhn, Lawhorn, Muse, Queen, Rennick, Reilly, Savage, Teel, Webb, Weber and More! United States: Meredith Music Publications, 2020. Page 33.

Practice

Excellence is not an accident. It's the result of a deliberate choice—a commitment to focused practice and lifelong learning. Embrace the journey, and you'll achieve levels of performance and impact that once seemed unattainable.

Action Steps:

1. **Set Clear Goals:** Identify the specific skills you want to improve, such as vocal shading, body language, or storytelling techniques.

2. **Seek Feedback:** Work with a coach, mentor, or trusted colleague to gain actionable insights. Incorporate their suggestions to refine your approach.

3. **Practice with Purpose:** Break down complex tasks into smaller components and focus on refining each element before integrating them.

4. **Rehearse Out Loud:** Simulate real scenarios to uncover areas for improvement. Use rehearsals to adjust pacing, tone, and flow.

5. **Reflect and Adjust:** After each performance or presentation, review what worked and what didn't. Use those insights to shape your next practice session.

6. **Commit to Continuous Growth:** View every opportunity—whether successful or not—as a chance to learn and improve.

Chapter Forty-four

Speechmaking Secrets I Learned from a DIY Bathroom Makeover

In the quiet sanctuary of my home, amidst the clatter of tools and the hum of transformation, I found myself undertaking an ambitious project: a bathroom remodel. Each tile I laid, each fixture I secured, felt like crafting a piece of art. It was a journey that mirrored the art of speechmaking—a blend of vision, preparation, and the willingness to embrace imperfection.

As Dale Carnegie once observed, *"There are always three speeches for every one you actually gave: the one you practiced, the one you gave, and the one you wish you gave."* (page 221) This triad of expression resonated deeply with my remodeling experience. Every element of the process, much like crafting a presentation, unfolded in three distinct phases.

The first was the vision—the flawless sanctuary I imagined before the first tool touched the space. In my mind, every detail aligned perfectly. The tiles gleamed, the fittings shone, and my novice hands executed the work with the precision of a seasoned artisan. This was the speech of dreams, practiced in solitude, untouched by the unpredictable nature of reality.

The second was the reality—the tangible result of my efforts. Here, imperfections emerged, visible perhaps only to me. A tile slightly misaligned, a corner not quite square. It was an honest reflection of effort and circumstance, much like a delivered presentation where nerves and unforeseen challenges might cause moments of hesitation. Yet, it was real. It existed beyond the realm of planning, a testament to the work I had done.

Finally, the third was the retrospective—the lessons learned and the lingering 'what ifs.' What if I had chosen a different pattern? What if I had started with a better plan? These were the whispers of hindsight, revealing a mosaic of missed opportunities and untapped potential. It was the presentation of reflection, replaying in the quiet moments, offering insights for the future.

And therein lay the most profound lesson: growth lies in embracing the imperfections of the second phase and learning from the reflections of the third. Just as I wouldn't tear down my bathroom to correct every flaw, I can't recapture the fleeting moments of a presentation already delivered. But I can carry those lessons forward, continuously refining my craft.

In the end, what remains is not just a remodeled bathroom or a presentation delivered, but a deeper understanding of our abilities. True perfection isn't the absence of flaws; it's the ability to see beauty in imperfection and the wisdom to grow from every experience.

Action Steps:

1. **Visualize Your Ideal Outcome:** Before starting a project or preparing a presentation, take time to envision the perfect result. Let this guide your preparation without becoming an unattainable standard.

2. **Embrace the Reality:** Understand that imperfections are part of the process. Recognize them as a reflection of effort rather than failure.

3. **Reflect and Learn:** After each experience, take time to analyze what worked, what didn't, and what you'd do differently next time.

4. **Seek Feedback:** Invite trusted peers or mentors to offer constructive input, whether it's on your presentation or your DIY project.

5. **Celebrate Progress:** Focus on how far you've come rather than dwelling on imperfections. Progress is a journey, not a destination.

6. **Apply the Lessons:** Use insights from past efforts to enhance future endeavors, whether in speaking, home projects, or any other area of growth.

Epilogue: The Journey Continues

Congratulations on reaching the end of this portion of your journey. But let's be clear—this is just the beginning of your transformation. Throughout this book, we've uncovered the building blocks of Executive Presence, the power of storytelling, and the art of impactful communication. We've delved into the nuances of leadership, influence, and legacy. Along the way, you've discovered how excelling at Executive Presence and strategic storytelling empowers you to authentically connect, inspire action, and leave a lasting impact. Now, you're equipped with the tools, techniques, and frameworks to elevate your presence and amplify your influence.

What You've Gained

Let's take a moment to reflect on what you've achieved and how far you've come:

1. **Built a Strong Foundation in the Fundamentals of Executive Presence**

You've learned to project confidence without arrogance, to balance authority with approachability, and to stay composed under pressure. These foundational skills now position you as a steady and reliable force in any professional setting.

2. **Enhanced Communication Skills**

You've developed storytelling techniques that turn abstract ideas into compelling narratives. You can now communicate complex concepts with clarity and adapt your style to resonate with any audience.

3. **Elevated Leadership Impact**

You've embraced authenticity, leading with integrity and vulnerability. You've harnessed emotional intelligence to connect deeply with your team, fostering trust, loyalty, and psychological safety.

4. **Commanded the Room**

Your presence speaks before you do. By honing non-verbal communication and responding with grace under high-stakes conditions, you've become the kind of leader people gravitate toward.

5. **Amplified Influence Across Organizations**

You've learned to align your leadership style with organizational goals, inspiring engagement, collaboration, and innovation. Your influence extends beyond the immediate, shaping a legacy others will follow.

6. **Leveraged Storytelling to Inspire Action**

You've discovered the art of combining data and narrative, using stories to connect emotionally, inspire action, and reinforce your vision.

7. **Navigated Challenges with Grace**

You've built resilience and adaptability, thriving in dynamic environments and turning crises into opportunities for growth.

8. **Achieved Long-Term Growth**

Practical tools and exercises have helped you refine your presence, ensuring you remain impactful and relevant as a leader.

9. **Built a Personal Legacy**

Your leadership is no longer just about today. You're mentoring others, championing meaningful causes, and building a reputation grounded in authenticity, integrity, and grace.

Your Next Steps

Now, as you close this book, I challenge you to turn what you've learned into action. Here's how:

1. **Practice Daily**: Each day presents an opportunity to refine your Executive Presence. Whether it's a meeting, a presentation, or a simple conversation, show up with confidence, composure, and authenticity.

2. **Seek Feedback**: Growth thrives on reflection. Regularly ask trusted colleagues and mentors for input on your communication, presence, and leadership style.

3. **Tell Your Story**: Use storytelling to connect, inspire, and motivate. Share your 'why' to align others with your vision and build lasting relationships.

4. **Measure Your Progress**: Keep a journal or tracker to document moments when you've applied what you've learned. Celebrate your wins and identify areas for continued improvement.

5. **Mentor Others**: Pass on your knowledge and help others grow. Leadership isn't just about your success; it's about building a legacy through the success of others.

The Journey Ahead

> *"Executive Presence is an endless journey. There's no finish line, only opportunities to grow and refine your impact as you continue."*

Executive Presence isn't a destination—it's a continuous evolution. Every interaction, challenge, and opportunity is a chance to grow stronger, to lead better, and to make a greater impact.

So, here's my final challenge to you: Stand in front of the mirror and ask yourself, *"What's the story I want to tell today?"* Then, step into the world and make it happen. Use the tools, frameworks, and insights from this book to elevate your leadership and inspire change. Your journey has only just begun—and the best is yet to come.

Thank you for letting me be a part of this transformation. Now, it's your turn to lead, to inspire, and to leave an indelible legacy.

Appendix A: Powerful Openers and Closers.

Anecdote

Ask for Imagination: *"Close your eyes and imagine you're standing on a cliff's edge, feeling the wind on your face..."*

Audience interaction: *"Raise your hand if you've ever felt like..."*

Challenge Assumptions: Challenge the status quo to spark curiosity and engagement.

Contradiction: Begin with a statement that contradicts popular belief to grab attention.

Controversial, powerful, or shocking statement: Shock your audience with a powerful, unexpected fact or claim.

Create empathy: Invite empathy by posing a question that resonates personally.

Cultural or popular reference

Current Event: Refer to a recent news story to make your topic timely and relevant.

Date: *"January 15, 2009."*

Define a term in your unique way

Demonstrate something

Direct challenge: Directly challenge your audience to engage with your topic more critically.

Historical Reference: Use history to add depth and significance to your message.

Humor: Use humor thoughtfully to connect and ease into your topic.

Interactive Technology: Use a live poll or digital interaction to engage the audience immediately.

Key question, or a connected series of questions, including with interaction: Pose a powerful question or series of questions to spark thought and interaction.

Metaphor, analogy, or simile

Mystery: *"There's a secret I've been wanting to share..."*

Name: Start with a meaningful or unexpected name to intrigue your audience.

Paint a picture of the future

Personal revelation: Share a personal revelation to foster connection.

Physical Action: Start with a dramatic or relevant physical movement.

Place: For example, *"Tampa Stadium. Tampa, Florida."*

Poem, riddle, or nursery rhyme

Powerful Imagery: *"Imagine a world where every single drop of water is as precious as gold."*

Powerful language

Prop: [Holding up an unusual object] *"You might be wondering why I have this with me today..."*

Quiz

Quote a powerful statement: (Quote first, then say who first said it.)

Quote a recent research report.

Quote an influential person: (Say the person's name first.) A carefully selected quote can set the stage for your topic. However, ensure that it's relevant and not overly used.

Refer to a recent conversation

Refer to a recent testimonial, a customer or employee email, or other correspondence

Rhetorical Devices: Techniques like alliteration, repetition, or rhyme can be catchy and memorable when used right at the beginning. *"From the bustling streets of New York to the quiet corners of Montana, one thing remains consistent..."*

Singing, playing a musical instrument, juggling, or another talent

Sound or Music: Use a sound clip or a piece of music to set the mood or highlight your point.

Spark curiosity: *"Did you know that companies who invested in speech recognition have seen a 13% increase in ROI within just 3 years?"*

Startling, interesting, or industry statistic related to your topic

Story—the most powerful: *"When I was 10, I witnessed something that forever changed the way I see the world..."* Or tell an inspiring story of a well-known person.

The Whisper: Lower your voice dramatically to create an intimate or suspenseful mood.

Unexpected Object Reveal: Unveil an unusual or symbolic object to spark curiosity.

Vivid visual

Double or even triple your impact by combining multiple techniques—like telling a story and ending it with a powerful quote. Starting your story with specific details, such as a date, time, and place—or a date, place, and protagonist—instantly adds credibility and draws your audience in.

You-focused openers:

1. *"Do you remember a time when..."*

2. *"Do you remember the first/ last time you..."*

3. *"Have you ever wondered why..."*: A question to spark curiosity or reflection.

4. *"How does it feel when you realize..."*: Stir emotions and invite personal connection.

5. *"How often have ever tried to..."*: Create a sense of community and shared experience.

6. *"How often have you felt/ seen/ experienced..."*

7. *"If I were to ask you..."*

8. *"Imagine yourself in a situation where..."*: Encourage the audience to place themselves into a specific context.

9. *"In your experience..."*

10. *"It might interest, surprise/ amaze you/ to know/ learn/ discover..."*

11. *"Picture this: You're standing at..."*: Set the stage for a vivid mental image.

12. *"Think about a time when you wished you had..."*: A reflective question tied to a missed opportunity or desired action.

13. *"Think back to when you last felt frustrated/ upset/ happy/ enthusiastic/ disappointed."*

14. *"You might be surprised to learn..."*

15. *"What advice did your dad/ parents/ mother/ first boss give you?"*

16. *"What would it mean to you if you could..."*: Tap into the audience's aspirations or desires.

17. *"What would you do if..."*: A hypothetical question that invites engagement.

18. *"When was the first or last time you..."*

19. *"You can feel confident..."*

20. *"What if I told you..."*

Anticipation openers:

1. **"Are you ready"**: Ask the audience to prepare to dive deep into the unknown.

2. **"Believe it or not"**: Build curiosity by revealing a hidden truth.

3. **"Brace yourself"**: Add a dramatic flair to prepare the audience for a revelation.

Appendix

4. *"Close your eyes and picture this"*: Add a sensory element to increase engagement.

5. *"Envision"*: Invite the audience to imagine a place where your idea comes to life.

6. *"Ever wondered"*: Pose a question to spark curiosity about how a phenomenon began.

7. *"Get ready to uncover"*: A directive that builds anticipation.

8. *"Guess what"*: Build suspense about what the future holds.

9. *"Have you ever dreamed of..."*: Tap into the audience's imagination and aspirations.

10. *"Hold onto your seats"*: Prepare the audience to discover something exciting.

11. *"I promise you"*: Assure the audience they will see things differently by the end of the presentation.

12. *"Imagine"*: Paint a picture of a world shaped by your vision.

13. *"In a moment"*: Tease the audience about a secret they're about to learn.

14. *"In just a few moments"*: A teaser that hints at a payoff later in the presentation.

15. *"Let's journey"*: Invite the audience to revisit a moment in history or an idea.

16. *"Picture this"*: Set a vivid scene to captivate the audience's imagination.

17. *"Prepare to be amazed"*: Promise the audience an inspiring story.

18. *"What if I told you..."*: A mysterious opening that sparks intrigue.

Remembrance Openers:

1. "As we come together today, we are united by the memories that bring both tears and smiles."

2. "As we come together, let's take a moment to remember and honor the indelible memories of..."

3. "As we stand together, let's take a journey through the cherished memories and lasting legacy of..."

4. "In every story told and memory shared today, we keep their spirit alive."

5. "In the echoing silence of remembrance, we come together to honor the life of..."

6. "In the gentle hush of this moment, we remember the profound impact of..."

7. "In the quiet reflections of today, we honor and remember the unforgettable moments we shared with..."

8. "It's said that life is a collection of moments. Today, we recall the special moments we shared with..."

9. "Let us begin by paying tribute to the memories that forever resonate in our hearts..."

10. "Let us honor not just the life that was, but the love that continues to surround us."

11. "Memories are the threads that bind us, and today, we weave together the tapestry of..."

12. "The footprints of a life well-lived never truly fade away. Today, we walk beside those footprints, remembering and honoring..."

13. "The true measure of a life is the impact it leaves on others. Today, we are testament to the profound impact of..."

14. "There are some who bring a light so bright to the world that even after they've gone, their light remains. Today, we remember such a light..."

15. "They say that to live in the hearts of those we leave behind is not to die. Today, we remember with gratitude and love..."

16. "Though they may no longer be with us, their legacy endures in the lives they've touched."

17. "Time may pass and fade away, but memories of our loved ones remain embedded in our hearts. Today, we gather to remember and honor..."

18. "Today, we celebrate a life that was a gift to all who knew them."

19. "Today, we gather not to mourn the loss, but to celebrate the life and legacy of..."

20. "With heavy hearts and fond memories, we come together to celebrate the life of..."

When choosing an opening, always consider your audience and the context. What works for one audience or situation might not work for another. Tailor your opening to be relevant, appropriate, and engaging for the people you are addressing, and the message you are conveying.

Appendix B: Outline for Crafting a Story:

Objective: Create a compelling story about one person facing a pivotal moment that leads to transformation, realization, or revelation. Incorporate these elements to ensure the story is engaging, relatable, and emotionally impactful.

Template:

1. **Set the Stage (Background):**

   - Who is the central character? (Provide their name, role, and a few details about their personality, values, or struggles).
   - What is their "normal" or status quo before the critical moment?
   - What were their beliefs, fears, or desires before this moment?
   - What are they seeking, fearing, or avoiding?

2. **The Inciting Incident (Catalyst):**

   - Describe the event, obstacle, or decision that pushes the character out of their comfort zone or that sets the story in motion. This is the moment their world is *"thrown out of whack."*
   - What unexpected challenge, problem, or observation forces them to face change? What disrupted the ordinary flow of events and forced a response?

3. **The Journey (Challenges and Obstacles):**

   - What small but increasing obstacles made the situation more difficult? How did they test the character's resolve or values?
   - Outline the increasing challenges, doubts, or decisions the character faces on their path to transformation.
   - Include any allies, mentors, or antagonists that shape their journey. What lessons or conflicts arise?

- How are their values, beliefs, or assumptions tested?

4. **The Critical Moment (Transformation, Realization, or Revelation):**

- What is the single, defining moment where everything changes for the character? One small event or decision that felt significant or surprising at the time—an insight, a choice, or a realization?
- Is it an internal realization (shift in mindset or perspective) or an external decision (action taken)?
- Describe the emotions involved—fear, joy, sadness, surprise—and make it vivid.

5. **The Aftermath (Resolution and Reflection):**

- How does the character navigate the "new normal" after this moment?
- What is the immediate consequence or long-term change in their understanding, behavior, or worldview? How did the character think, feel, or act differently afterward?

6. **Reflect on the Universal Insight:**

- Reflect on the lesson or universal insight the audience can take away.
- What does this story teach about leadership, change, decision-making, or the human experience?

7. **Sensory and Emotional Details:**

- What sights, sounds, smells or emotions made this moment memorable for you?
- Emphasize the emotional undercurrent to ensure the audience connects deeply with the story.

Additional Notes:
- Use ordinary, relatable moments as the foundation. Avoid grand or unrelatable scenarios like climbing Mount Everest.
- Focus on subtle but profound insights or small, critical decisions that resonate universally.

- Ensure the story flows naturally, using conversational language and varying sentence structure for pacing.
- The critical moment should occur near the end, with the beginning and resolution acting as bookends.

Example Story Seeds:

- A business executive who, during a crucial merger meeting, has a sudden realization about their company's values.
- A simple moment—like finding a family recipe—that sparks reflection on lost traditions or connections.
- A leader who fails a small task, but discovers an invaluable lesson about trust and delegation.

Appendix C: Hand Gestures for Executive Presence and Presentation Skills

Negative Gestures to Avoid

Understanding and avoiding certain hand positions can help presenters maintain confidence, engagement, and authority.

1. The Fig Leaf
   - **What it is**: Resting your hands together low in front of you.
   - **Why it's negative**: Signals nervousness or lack of confidence.

2. The Flashing Fig Leaf
   - **What it is**: Repeatedly moving hands up and down from the fig leaf position.
   - **Why it's negative**: Distracting and emphasizes anxiety.

3. The Military Stance
   - **What it is**: Hands clasped behind the back.
   - **Why it's negative**: Creates an overly rigid or intimidating presence.

4. The Prayer Position
   - **What it is**: Hands clasped together in front of the chest.
   - **Why it's negative**: May seem desperate or anxious.

5. The Pockets
   - **What it is**: Hands tucked into pockets.
   - **Why it's negative**: Suggests disengagement or insecurity.

6. The Hip Grip
   - **What it is**: Hands on hips with elbows pointing outward.
   - **Why it's negative**: Conveys aggression or a domineering attitude.

7. The Over-Gesturer
- **What it is**: Excessive or exaggerated hand movements.
- **Why it's negative**: Overwhelms the audience and detracts from your message.
8. Pointing at the Audience
- **What it is**: Using a pointed finger toward the crowd.
- **Why it's negative**: Can feel confrontational or accusatory.
9. Touching the Face or Neck
- **What it is**: Fidgeting with the face, hair, or neck.
- **Why it's negative**: Reflects nervousness or discomfort.
10. Crossed Arms
- **What it is**: Arms folded across the chest.
- **Why it's negative**: Creates a barrier, signaling defensiveness or disinterest.

Positive Gestures to Enhance Executive Presence

Using purposeful and appropriate gestures reinforces credibility, connection, and confidence.

1. Open Palms
- **What to do**: Hold hands open, palms facing the audience.
- **Conveys**: Honesty and approachability.
2. Natural Movements
- **What to do**: Allow hands to move rhythmically with speech.
- **Conveys**: Authenticity and comfort.
3. Steepling
- **What to do**: Touch fingertips together lightly.
- **Conveys**: Confidence and thoughtfulness.
4. Wide Gestures
- **What to do**: Spread arms wide to discuss expansive ideas.
- **Conveys**: Enthusiasm and optimism.

5. Counting with Fingers
- **What to do**: Raise fingers sequentially while listing points.
- **Conveys**: Organization and clarity.

6. Illustrating Size or Scale
- **What to do**: Use hands to demonstrate magnitude or dimensions.
- **Conveys**: Visual engagement and clarity.

7. Reaching Toward the Audience
- **What to do**: Extend hands slightly forward, palms up.
- **Conveys**: Inclusion and connection.

8. Gentle Tapping of the Chest
- **What to do**: Lightly touch the chest with an open hand.
- **Conveys**: Passion and sincerity.

9. Small Circular Motions
- **What to do**: Make circular movements to indicate ongoing processes.
- **Conveys**: Continuity and harmony.

10. Pointing Up or Out (Sparingly)
- **What to do**: Use a finger to highlight key ideas.
- **Conveys**: Authority and focus.

Practice Tips

Developing effective hand gestures requires deliberate practice.

- **Record Yourself**: Identify natural and effective movements by watching recordings of your presentations.
- **Use a Mirror**: Practice in front of a mirror to align gestures with tone and content.
- **Purposeful Gestures**: Ensure gestures support and emphasize your words without overwhelming the audience.

Appendix D: Secrets for Memorizing Text

Memorizing text becomes easier when you focus on distilling it to its core meaning. By systematically paring down the content, you isolate the most critical words and concepts, eliminating distractions and sharpening your understanding. This method isn't just about reducing word count—it's about internalizing the essence of the text. With each pass, you remove unnecessary words like articles or prepositions, then fill in the gaps mentally, reinforcing your ability to recall the material. Over time, this practice helps you transition from relying on a full script to recalling the key points naturally and confidently. Here's what you should consider eliminating:

1. **Articles**: Words like "a," "an," and "the" are often unnecessary for understanding the main ideas.

2. **Prepositions**: Words such as "in," "on," "at," "from," "with," "about," "against," etc., can usually be omitted without losing the essential meaning.

3. **Conjunctions**: Words like "and," "but," "or," "so," "yet," and "for" often serve to connect clauses but aren't essential when listing key points.

4. **Auxiliary (Helping) Verbs**: Verbs like "is," "are," "was," "were," "be," "being," "been," "do," "does," "did," "have," "has," "had" can be dropped to focus on the main action verbs.

5. **Non-Essential Adjectives and Adverbs**: Descriptive words that don't add critical information can be eliminated. Keep only those that are vital to the main idea.

6. **Pronouns**: Words like "he," "she," "it," "they," "this," "that" can often be removed or replaced with the nouns they refer to for clarity.

7. **Interjections and Filler Words**: Words or phrases like "well," "you know," "basically," "actually," which don't add substantive meaning.

Focus on Retaining:

- **Nouns**: The main subjects and objects that are central to the text.
- **Main Verbs**: Action words that drive the meaning.
- **Essential Adjectives/Adverbs**: Only if they are crucial for understanding.

Example:

Original Text:

"The quick brown fox jumps over the lazy dog."

Key Words:

"Quick brown fox jumps over lazy dog."

Further Simplified:

"Fox jumps over dog."

In this example, you can decide whether adjectives like "quick," "brown," "lazy" are essential for your understanding or memorization. If they are, keep them; if not, they can be omitted.

Another Example:

Original Text:

"During the annual conference, leading experts in neuroscience discussed the future of brain-computer interfaces."

Key Words:

"Annual conference, leading neuroscience experts discussed future brain-computer interfaces."

Further Simplified:

"Conference: neuroscience experts on brain-computer interfaces future."

Tips:

- **Be Selective with Adjectives/Adverbs:** Only keep them if they change the meaning significantly.

- **Use Abbreviations or Symbols:** If appropriate, to represent words or concepts.

- **Organize Logically:** Arrange key words in a way that makes sense to you, possibly in bullet points or mind maps.

By systematically removing non-essential words, you'll create a concise version of the text that highlights the main ideas, making it easier to memorize.

About the author

For over three decades, Bob Roitblat has been a steadfast innovator and strategist, skillfully captaining more than a dozen businesses through the tempestuous tides of entrepreneurship. As a seasoned helmsman steering the course of profit and loss, he has weathered the storms of financial uncertainty, and navigated companies through every stage of their life cycle, from their maiden voyage to their final sunset cruise.

Bob's extensive experience spans a vast ocean of diverse industries, including high technology, distribution, construction, manufacturing, and professional services. His expertise, like a beacon guiding sailors through treacherous waters, is also sought by governmental and non-governmental agencies, as well as educational institutions.

Throughout his career, Bob has played an instrumental role in the successful sale of numerous businesses, adeptly charting a course through the intricacies of mergers and acquisitions like an experienced yachtsman in churning seas. Additionally, he has orchestrated several impressive turnarounds, skillfully righting capsized ventures.

Bob likens the world of business to the realm of yacht racing — his hobby, if you haven't noticed. He asserts that both spheres demand leadership, teamwork, and a capacity for swift ideation and decision-making. Leveraging this analogy, he provides eloquent and insightful guidance to leaders, helping them develop pragmatic and proven business skills effective in driving business transformation, irrespective of whether they are operating in a calm environment or amidst raging market storms.

With an unwavering passion for helping leaders become victorious skippers, and a wealth of hands-on experience, Bob serves as an exceptional mentor. He guides clients in developing a goal-oriented mindset and sharpening the competitive skills essential for achieving enduring success. Moreover, he helps them become the kind of leaders that others not only respect but eagerly follow, like loyal crew members.

Influence Amplified

Before being drawn to the irresistible call of sea, Bob was drawn to storytelling and the promise of adventure in the movie industry. Eager to participate, he directed his first TV commercial at the age of 16, and through a combination of happenstance and luck, he went on to appear as a principal actor or co-star in over 60 TV shows and feature films—often portraying a villain. Bob also lent his talents as a writer, producer, and director to various projects, all while continuing to helm his numerous businesses.

Although he no longer appears in films, Bob maintains his acting and directing prowess by helping others become spellbinding storytellers and persuasive presenters.

Acknowledgements

When the credits roll at the end of a movie, it's easy to tune out. But if you actually sit through them, it's fascinating to see just how many people played a role in bringing that story to life—lighting crews, sound editors, costume designers, and a long list of others whose names most of us will never know.

Writing a book doesn't require a cinematographer or a gaffer, but it's far from a solo act. Along the way, so many people shape the process, offer insights, and sometimes—without even realizing it—become part of the story themselves. To each and every one of them, I'm deeply grateful.

A special thanks to Stephen Shapiro for his guidance on writing, production, and distribution tools. And to Michael Fornwald—who, unknowingly, became a test subject for many of the ideas explored in these pages. Their contributions made a real difference.

Finally, to every group that invited me to keynote or facilitate a workshop—thank you. Each opportunity helped me refine my craft, and for that, I'm truly appreciative.

www.ingramcontent.com/pod-product-compliance
Lightning Source LLC
LaVergne TN
LVHW021655060526
838200LV00050B/2367